A M E R I C A N
P R O F I L E S

Twentieth-Century Writers

1900–1950

∎

Tom Verde

Facts On File
New York

For my
Mother and Father

Twentieth-Century Writers 1900–1950

Copyright © 1993 by Tom Verde

Facts On File, Inc.
460 Park Avenue South
New York NY 10016
USA

Library of Congress Cataloging-in-Publication Data
Verde, Thomas A. (Thomas Aquinas), 1958–
    Twentieth-century writers 1900–1950 / Tom Verde.
      p.   cm. — (American profiles)
    Includes bibliographical references and index.
    Summary: A collection of short literary biographies covering the major American fiction writers of the first half of the twentieth century, including Jack London, Sherwood Anderson, and John Steinbeck.
    ISBN 0-8160-2573-8
    1. Authors, American—20th century—Biography—Juvenile literature. [1. Authors, American.] I. Title. II. Series: American profiles (Facts On File, Inc.)
PS129.V47   1992
813'.5209—dc20
[B]   92-19075

A British CIP catalogue record for this book is available from the British Library.

Facts On File books are available at special discounts when purchased in bulk quantities for businesses, associations, institutions or sales promotions. Please contact our Special Sales Department in New York at 212/683-2244 (dial 800/322-8755 except in NY, AK or HI) or in Oxford at 865/728399.

Series interior and jacket design by Ron Monteleone
Composition by Facts On File, Inc.
Manufactured by the Maple-Vail Book Manufacturing Group
Printed in the United States of America

10 9 8 7 6 5 4 3 2 1

This book is printed on acid-free paper.

Contents

Acknowledgments

*T*he author would like to gratefully acknowledge the loving support of his family, Kate and Sam, without whose personal sacrifices this project could never have been completed. Deep appreciation also goes to the author's friend and editor, James Warren, for his kind patience and understanding; to friend and colleague, Pat Tracey, for his legwork; to the English Department at the Waynflete School for its guidance; and to Madge Kaplan and WGBH for the eleventh-hour rescue.

Thanks also go to the following institutions for providing illustrations:

The National Archives
The Library of Congress
Nebraska State Historical Society
The John F. Kennedy Library
Random House
University of Virginia Library

Introduction

*T*he period of American literary history covered in this book was a time of tremendous growth and change in this country and, indeed, the world.

In the year of Jack London's birth, 1876, a horse and buggy was still the way to get around town, people lit their homes with gaslights, and an impetuous army colonel by the name of Custer made his last stand on a lonely hill by the Little Bighorn River in what is now southern Montana.

When John Steinbeck died in 1968, superhighways instead of wagon trails crisscrossed the continental United States, worldwide communication had become an everyday fact of life, and human beings were within a year of setting foot on the moon.

In between came two world wars, a crippling economic depression along with a remarkable recovery, the growth of industries and labor unions, the development of the modern city and its surrounding suburbs, the advancement of civil rights, the harnessing of atomic energy and the invention of nuclear weapons.

This progress was fueled by the spirit of "Manifest Destiny," a 19th-century concept embraced by Americans who believed it was their divine right to lay claim to all the land between the Atlantic and Pacific oceans, from the Canadian border to the Rio Grande.

Although we now realize that this attitude was environmentally insensitive and flagrantly disregarded what we would now define as the human rights of the indigenous peoples who were here before the Europeans came, the philosophy of Manifest Destiny came to define the restless (some said imperialist) nature of American culture—one forever changing, growing and moving forward in a wave of technological progress.

Significant shifts in the focus of American literature followed in the wake of 19th-century American expansionism across the heartlands, the plains, the mountains and the desert. With the exception of James Fenimore Cooper, whose work was inspired by the frontier movement, American writers of the 19th century wrote mostly about life back East. Early 20th-century American writers took on the task of chronicling the country's growing pains as it emerged from an isolated union of states and territories to become a world power.

We can trace this history by reading the works of the writers in this book and of this period. We can follow Jack London to the edges of the Alaskan wilderness—the last American frontier—and over the high seas, where a new type of literary hero, the individualist, grapples with the powers of nature. We can accompany Willa Cather's immigrant pioneer families across the plains and appreciate their contribution to the nation's cultural "melting pot." We may gaze through a literary magnifying glass at the changing nature of life in the small midwestern towns of Sherwood Anderson's imagination. We may wander through the dark world of William Faulkner's South or witness the suffering of migrant workers and the stunning beauty of the Pacific coast through John Steinbeck's eyes. We are privy to the world of the privileged class thanks to F. Scott Fitzgerald, and we appreciate what it is to be an American abroad in the books of Ernest Hemingway.

If there is a common thread in this tapestry of the American experience, it is that literature was becoming more available to the middle and lower classes. Formerly the almost exclusive property of the wealthy and the university-educated, literature was beginning to reflect and deal with the social upheavals taking place at the time.

Labor unions, public welfare, public works, public education—these were all conceived in the first half of the 20th century, a time in which the middle class emerged as a powerful economic and social force in this country. It is only fitting, then, that the period outlined in this volume begins and ends with the lives of two very active social-ists—Jack London and Richard Wright.

"American writers never have a second act," F. Scott Fitzgerald once said. In so far as the eight writers in this book each made at least one major contribution to the body of American literature and its future, this may be true. Many, in fact, struggled unsuccessfully to escape being pigeonholed by critics and the reading public, who based their judgments solely on the popularity of a single work.

This book attempts to introduce the reader to the lives of these writers and to provide a small measure of insight into their work. A fuller understanding can be gained by reading those works them-selves. In doing so, one may come to realize that each reputation rests on more than a single best-seller. It may even become evident that these writers were all courageous innovators in the field of American letters.

Jack London
(1876–1916)

Sailor, gold prospector, adventurer, hobo, war correspondent
and world traveler—writer Jack London was also the most
commercially successful American author
of his time.
(National Archives)

*I*n the year 1849, San Francisco, California, was nothing but a small coastal village. By the end of 1850, it was a bustling, thriving city of 25,000 thanks to the '49 California gold rush. In the wake of the Civil War, as people moved west across the Great Plains, the new city attracted pioneers, prospectors, businessmen, cowboys, criminals and faith healers of every kind. Along its muddy streets you could purchase the latest perfume from Paris or the newest potion to make your hair grow.

This was the world into which Jack London was born on January 12, 1876. London spent his childhood and early teen years in bitter poverty and unhappiness. His mother was often cruel and emotionally unavailable; his father had abandoned them both and denied that he was even responsible for London's birth; his schoolmaster was a drunkard who beat him.

When his stepfather lost his job as a night watchman London became the breadwinner in the family at 11 years of age, holding down two paper routes, working in an ice house on Saturdays and a bowling alley on Sundays.

One bright spot in his boyhood was the Oakland Public Library, where a kindly librarian introduced him to the works of such writers as Horatio Alger, Washington Irving, Herman Melville, Gustave Flaubert, Leo Tolstoy and Dostoevsky. Although the librarian encouraged London to continue his studies, poverty and the needs of his family forced him to work 10- to 13-hour days for 10 cents an hour in a canning factory instead of going on to high school.

He finally got fed up and became an "oyster pirate" on the San Francisco Bay, robbing the privately-owned oyster beds by night and unloading his booty at the wharfs the next morning.

Here in this shady and dangerous environment, London developed a taste for whisky. One night, in a drunken stupor, he fell off the docks and almost drowned drifting out to sea. After being rescued by a fishing boat he decided to turn over a new leaf and joined the State Fish Patrol, hunting down and capturing his former pirate comrades.

In the winter of 1892, he shipped out on the *Sophie Sutherland*, a seal boat bound for the icy hunting grounds off the Siberian coast. Life on board the *Sophie Sutherland* was a lot tougher than on the docks of Oakland and the 17-year-old London found that aggression meant survival. These experiences provided material for one of his most popular books, *The Sea Wolf* (1904).

Back in the Bay area in the summer of 1893, London grudgingly took a job in a mill in order to help his family. At the unusually supportive suggestion of his mother, he entered a story contest at the San Francisco *Morning Call* and won the first prize of $25.

His story was an account of surviving a typhoon off the Japanese coast on board the *Sophie Sutherland*. The editor of the *Call* loved

London's vivid and powerful descriptions of the mountainous, slate-gray seas of the North Pacific. He was also impressed with the rhythm of the piece, which rolled and dipped with the waves. It was an impressive first effort for a writer of London's age.

London spent a year bumming around the country on freight trains, and was converted to socialism by reading Karl Marx's *Communist Manifesto*. As a struggling member of the working class himself, he identified with Marx's philosophy and dedicated his life to social change.

Certain now that his calling in life was to be a writer, and determined to climb out of the "Social Pit" of poverty, London decided he needed a better education. But school wasn't the place for a restless soul like London, and he got the urge to roam again one day in 1897, when he opened the newspaper and read about a gold rush in the Yukon Territory of Canada. Thousands of American men had caught "gold fever" and were abandoning their homes, their jobs and their families to head for the frozen regions of the North.

Grubstaked by his sister Eliza, London set out on the long, grueling trek to the Klondike, first by boat to Alaska, then by foot along the Chilkoot Pass, bearing a 150-pound pack on his back. He reached the Yukon as winter set in and holed up in a cabin with several other Klondikers.

"It was in the Klondike that I found myself," London later said. "There nobody talks. Everybody thinks. You get your perspective. I got mine."

Surrounded by the awesome beauty of the "white silence," London came to appreciate the power and integrity of nature, as Kaori O'Connor has observed in her introduction to London's *The Cruise of the Snark* (1911). Although it could be cruel and unforgiving, there was a sense of crude justice in nature, far nobler than anything he had seen in the so-called civilized world where the underprivileged suffered at the hands of the upper classes. Here, class meant nothing. What mattered was skill, instinct, strength, courage and self-reliance.

By the time London reached Dawson, the region's gold capital, the boom was over. He spent a few months in the saloons listening to old-time prospectors tell their stories. Then, broke and sick with scurvy, he got on a small boat with two companions and floated down the Yukon 1,700 miles to the sea. Back home in San Francisco in August of 1898, he was ready to write.

The time, as Kaori O'Connor points out, was precisely right for London. During the mid- to late 19th century, literature in America was largely a preoccupation of the privileged East Coast society. It explored upper-class values, was often sentimental and overloaded with conventional morality. Stylistically, it was as stuffy and ornate as the Victorian drawing rooms where it was

Alaska's Chilkoot Pass, 1897. Hundreds of men—including London—followed this treacherous trail through the mountains in search of gold. London's experiences there inspired him to write The Call of the Wild *and many other Klondike stories.*
(Library of Congress)

meant to be read aloud. For the most part, it was unrealistic and out of touch with the sweeping changes that were occurring in the American landscape, such as the rapid growth of cities and industry, and the bold, sweeping settlement of the western half of the country.

A few publishers, however, began to recognize that there was a huge, untapped reading market in the working class, and so a new breed of "popular" magazine was born. Inexpensive, packed with short stories, serializations and features, these magazines catered to the tastes of the man on the street.

London's unique blend of realism and adventure was what the new reading public wanted. His first sale of "To the Man on Trail" (1899) was quickly followed up by another, "The White Silence" (1899), a tale of brutish survival and the struggle of man against nature, featuring the Malemute Kid, a hard-bitten, seasoned veteran of the North. London now began to sell his stories regularly to the popular magazines, but his biggest break undoubtedly came when he sold the lengthy "An Odyssey of the North" (1900) to the prestigious *Atlantic Monthly* for the princely sum of $120.

This story of an Eskimo seal hunter who leaves his wife and her kidnapper/lover to die in the frozen Yukon was shocking and unfamiliar material to the cultured readership of *The Atlantic Monthly*. In contrast to the polite and predictable figures of drawing-room fiction, London's characters were well-rounded, impassioned men and women, struggling violently against their environment and with each other. His powerful themes and prose soon caught the attention of the editors at the Boston publishing house of Houghton Mifflin, and they offered him a contract for a collection of his short stories.

The publication of *The Son of the Wolf* (1900) brought London great popularity and critical success. He was hailed as "the Kipling of the North" and came to the notice of publisher S. S. McClure. McClure began printing London's stories in his magazine *McClure's*, and also published London's second story collection, *The God of His Fathers* (1901).

London then married Bess Maddern and moved to Oakland. Bess gave birth to a daughter, Joan, in January of 1901—much to London's disappointment, since he was hoping for a boy. A second daughter, Bess, was born in 1902. Also that year, London met a Macmillan editor, George P. Brett, who published another collection of Klondike stories, *Children of the Frost*, while Century came out with *Cruise of the Dazzler*, a juvenile book. Brett, a remarkably understanding editor with deep pockets and endless patience, played a significant role in London's life.

London was on his way to South Africa for the American Press Association to write a series of reports on the aftermath of the Boer War when his assignment was cancelled. He took advantage of the opportunity to tour the slums of the East End of London, and he wrote about the starvation and disease he saw there in *The People of the Abyss* (1903).

That he could follow up his immensely popular Klondike stories with a social tract on poverty is a good example of London's dedication to his political ideals. He has sometimes been compared to Mark Twain for becoming a literary sausage grinder, churning out story after story in pursuit of cash. Yet he would drop everything to write passionate social works like *The People of the Abyss* or *The Iron Heel* (1908), which had little commercial appeal. In the end, as biographer Richard O'Connor observes in his biography, *Jack London*, it became apparent that London simply wrote "because he wanted to."

Back home from Europe, at first with no intention of writing any more Klondike stories for a while, London then plunged into the book that would secure his place in American literature.

The Call of the Wild (1903) is the story of a domestic dog—half St. Bernard, half Scotch shepherd—named Buck, who is stolen from his home in California and made to serve as a sled dog in the Yukon. Exposed to the savage brutality of both men and dogs in this wilderness, Buck is forced to fight for his life until he is rescued by the humane John Thornton. When Thornton is murdered, Buck returns to the wild and becomes the leader of a pack of wolves.

On the one hand, *The Call of the Wild* is a story of initiation and the fragile nature of civilization's moral boundaries. Buck must learn how to survive in this unfamiliar world of cruel masters and sled dogs who have little regard for the lives of their fellows. But the book also celebrates a return to the nobility of the primitive world. Buck heeds the ancient call of the wild and in doing so is immortalized:

> When the long winter nights come on and the wolves follow their meat into the lower valleys, he may be seen running at the head of the pack through the pale moonlight or the glimmering borealis, leaping gigantic above his fellows, his great throat a-bellow as he sings a song of the younger world, which is the song of the pack.

Jack London

The Call of the Wild was a tremendous best-seller (the first printing of 10,000 copies sold out in a single day) and catapulted London into international prominence. Having become America's first popular writer, London was ultimately responsible for introducing literature to millions of people—mostly from the lower classes—who had never before taken much of an interest in reading.

His popularity also began to attract a variety of flatterers and hangers-on, one of whom was a plain but shapely 32-year-old spinster named Charmian Kittredge. She and London began to have an affair until finally London informed Bess that he was leaving her. He took a room in Oakland, and the scandal of his separation was splashed all over the front pages nationwide.

Despite *The Call of the Wild*'s good fortune, the book didn't make London rich. Having no idea that a story about a dog would be so successful and still desperately in need of cash, London had sold Macmillan all rights to the book for $2,000 in lieu of royalties. This plus another $2,000 or so (the accounts vary) from *The Saturday Evening Post* for the serialization rights would be all the money London would get for what is now recognized as an American classic. But $2,000 was more than he had ever earned before from his writing, and he took advantage of this brief period of financial security to begin the writing of another novel, *The Mercy of the Sea*, which became *The Sea Wolf*.

It is the story of a brutish but intelligent sea captain, Wolf Larsen, and his struggle for power with the intellectual Humphry Van Weyden on board the seal boat *Ghost*. Larsen rescues Van Weyden, a genteel literary critic and writer, from the sinking of a ferry in San Francisco Bay and presses him into service as a cabin boy. Forced to survive in the rugged environment (just as London had on board the *Sophie Sutherland*), Van Weyden becomes as tough as the crew, and the amused Larsen promotes him to first mate. Van Weyden challenges Larsen's authority, however, when the Ghost picks up the survivors from a wrecked ship. Among these survivors is the beautiful and delicate poetess Maud Brewster. (Brewster was obviously based on Charmian Kittredge; London wrote her into the story at about the same time he and Charmian began having their affair.)

Larsen and Van Weyden compete for Brewster's affections until she and the writer escape in a small boat and make it to an island. Larsen, his crew having deserted him, washes up on the island and soon dies.

In the character of Wolf Larsen, London was attempting to portray his own concept of a "superman" who is ultimately flawed by his own base desires.

"I am convinced that he is the perfect type of the primitive man," Van Weyden, the narrator, observes, "born a thousand years or generations too late and an anachronism in this culminating century of civilization."

London was also striving to produce a commercially popular novel and he succeeded. *The Sea Wolf* became a runaway best-seller, was widely praised by the critics for its blend of romance and realism, and was the basis of several films.

In January of 1904, London traveled to Japan and Korea as a correspondent for the Hearst newspapers in order to cover the Russo-Japanese war. He distinguished himself—and irritated his colleagues—by slipping into the forbidden war zone and filing the first report when the bullets started to fly between Russian and Japanese forces. Later that year he wrote *The Game*, a short novel about prizefighting.

In 1905, London finally divorced Bess and married Charmian. After buying a ranch near the village of Glen Ellen in Sonoma County, California's Valley of the Moon, he began to make plans for a cruise around the world. He went on a lecture tour to earn money for the trip and wrote a sequel to *The Call of the Wild, White Fang* (1906), which, as critic Richard O'Connor put it, was "twice as long" and "half as good" as its predecessor. The following year he began to build a schooner, the *Snark*, which eventually cost him $50,000.

Ever since he had read about them in Melville's *Typee* and in the tales of Robert Louis Stevenson, London had longed to visit the exotic islands of the South Pacific. After some initial delays in getting the *Snark* underway, he and Charmian set sail in April of 1907 on a voyage that would last over two years, with calls at Hawaii, the Marquesas, Tahiti and Australia. Along the way, London wrote the autobiographical novel *Martin Eden* (1909) and more stories for the magazines, including one of his most famous, "To Build a Fire" (1909). He also wrote an account of the journey, *The Cruise of the Snark*.

Although the trip was everything London had dreamed of, it had its share of nightmares. Hailing at the Marquesas—Polynesian islands that were Melville's setting for the novel *Typee*—London was shocked to find crippling poverty and disease afflicting the native people there. When the *Snark* reached Tahiti in January of

1908, London learned that he was in serious financial trouble. He had left Charmian's aunt in charge of his accounts, and she had completely bungled them, in addition to embezzling thousands of dollars. London had to interrupt his trip to return home and straighten things out.

Back in the South Seas, London and the crew of the *Snark* were plagued by fever, malaria, skin ulcers and jungle rot. By the time they made it to Australia, London had lost 10 layers of skin and had to be hospitalized for five weeks. The remainder of the trip was finally canceled, and in July of 1909, London and Charmian returned to California.

With the publication of *Martin Eden*, sales of London's novels began to decline. He took a stab at recapturing the book-buying market with *Burning Daylight* (1910), another novel of the Yukon, but since his books were often serialized in magazines, people were more willing to invest a few cents for a copy of *Cosmopolitan* or *The Saturday Evening Post* than a few dollars for a book they had already read.

Determined to make a comeback, London picked up his pace as a short story writer, putting in 19-hour days until his income climbed to $75,000 a year. Although that was an astronomical sum in those days, it was barely enough to keep London's creditors at bay. He had fallen into a cycle of earning large amounts of money, only to spend twice what he made on plans and investments that often blew up in his face.

He also suffered numerous personal tragedies during this period. His daughters rejected him, despite his attempts at a rapprochement. Charmian lost two babies, and she and London began to drift apart. He tried to give up alcohol in 1912 by going with Charmian on a four-month, sober cruise around Cape Horn, but resumed drinking when he got back. He wrote of his struggles with the bottle in *John Barleycorn* (1913).

In 1913 his appendix burst, and the surgeon who performed the appendectomy informed him that his kidneys were deteriorating. The climax came later that year when Wolf House, his magnificent, brand-new, $100,000 stone mansion, mysteriously burned to the ground a week before he was to move in. It was suspected, but never proven, that arson was the cause.

But London still had the will to work, and in 1914 he traveled to Mexico to report on the Revolution for *Collier's*. A severe bout of dysentery coupled with pleurisy forced him to return home, where the books that he continued to write unfortunately proved to be of little interest to the reading public.

His years cruising the high seas and holed up on his ranch had put him out of touch with what was happening in the rest of the world. America was changing. Cities were growing as never before, industry was pumping up the economy, and writers like Theodore Dreiser who chronicled these events were becoming more popular. London had come to be viewed as a writer of the bygone era of the gold rush. Most of his last major efforts—*The Mutiny of the Elsinore* (1914), *The Star Rover* (1915), *The Little Lady of the Big House* (1916)—went virtually unnoticed by the critics or the reading public.

In the winter of 1915, London—by then suffering from acute rheumatism—went with Charmian to Waikiki in the Hawaiian Islands (a favorite spot from their voyage on board the *Snark*), hoping that the warm, gentle climate would help restore his health.

He lived there for several months, happily working on his tales of the South Seas and relaxing. Ignoring the diet of fresh vegetables prescribed by his doctors, he gorged himself on raw fish, barbecued pork and alcohol until he suffered an attack brought on by his kidney disease. Strong doses of narcotics were needed to get him on his feet again.

He went back to Glen Ellen in July, then returned to Hawaii in January of 1916. A month later he resigned from the Socialist Party, disgusted with its lack of support for the Allies in World War I. After he returned to his California ranch in August of 1916, his health continued to decline. The years of alcohol abuse and overeating had taken their toll. His diseased kidneys were unable to cope with the poison spreading throughout his system. He suffered from constant headaches, agonizing uremia, nephritis, dysentery, crippling rheumatism and edema, which swelled his ankles. Thirty-five pounds overweight, he wandered about his ranch with a blank, morphine-induced stare on his flabby, colorless face. He had only just turned 40 years old.

Still, London had enough spirit left in him to think about getting his career moving again. In his final days, he spoke of making improvements to his ranch, of serializing his autobiography in the magazines, and of a trip to the Scandinavian countries to do research on Norse mythology for a historical novel he had in mind.

On the morning of November 22, 1916, London's Japanese valet couldn't rouse his master. He ran for Charmian who tried to get

Jack London

London near the end of his life at his ranch home in Sonoma County, California. Bloated, overweight and ravaged by disease, the dejected author spent his final days there, planning ways to get his career moving again. He died at Glen Ellen at 40 years of age.
(Library of Congress)

London up to drink some coffee, but the writer wouldn't respond; he had fallen into a coma. The doctor was called, and when he arrived he noticed two empty vials of morphine on the floor. Unable to stand the pain any longer, London had apparently attempted to take his life with an overdose.

A team of physicians tried all day long to rouse him from the coma but failed. He died at 7:45 that evening. Charmian insisted that publicly his death be attributed to natural causes. The doctors complied and listed "gastrointestinal type of uremia" as the cause. News of his death bumped the war dispatches off the front pages of American newspapers, and in Europe his obituary got more space than that of Franz Josef of Austria, who had died the previous day.

London is most remembered today for *The Call of the Wild*, *The Sea Wolf*, *White Fang* and a handful of his short stories set in the Yukon—mere drops in the bucket when stacked up against his entire canon, which includes almost 50 novels, several collections of short stories and two plays, plus numerous news dispatches and magazine articles.

Some critics who have delved deeply into his life have labeled him a "hack" rather than a literary artist. It is true that much of what he produced in the years after his cruise on the *Snark* was formulaic, and even London called himself a "brain merchant."

But this first great American writer of the 20th century ought to be remembered for more than this. Self-educated and self-made, rising above his poverty, London embodied the classic American success story of rags-to-riches. His distinctive, straightforward style of storytelling, and the realism of his subject matter, blew on the genteel, literary scene of the day with all the force of the typhoons he had steered through on the high seas. He became one of the principal crusaders for naturalism—a movement that depicted human life and society as objectively and truthfully as modern science treated its subjects.

In doing so, London personified the transition between the 19th and 20th century in American literature. He embraced the naturalism of Edgar Allan Poe, Stephen Crane and others, and passed it on to such later writers as Ernest Hemingway, William Faulkner and John Steinbeck.

Just as the ghost of his heroic dog Buck, in *The Call of the Wild*, may sometimes be heard bellowing in the distant wilderness, so do London's words continue to resound in American fiction.

Chronology

January 12, 1876	born in San Francisco, California
1891–92	graduates grammar school; works in a cannery to help support family; buys sloop for $300 and becomes "oyster pirate"
1893	sails to the North Pacific on board seal boat; wins essay contest writing about typhoon off the coast of Japan
1897–98	joins the Klondike gold rush; winters in a cabin in the Yukon
1900	"An Odyssey of the North" appears in *The Atlantic Monthly*; *The Son of the Wolf*, first collection of short stories; marries Bess Maddern
1903	*The Call of the Wild, The People of the Abyss*; begins affair with Charmian Kittredge
1904	travels to Japan and Korea to cover the Russo- Japanese war; *The Sea Wolf* is published and becomes best- seller
1905	marries Charmian; buys 130-acre ranch at Glen Ellen in Sonoma County, California
1906	begins building the schooner *Snark* for a trip around the world; *White Fang*, a sequel to *The Call of the Wild*
1907	sets out on a 27-month voyage with Charmian on board the *Snark*; visits Hawaii, the Marquesas, Tahiti and the Solomon Islands
1913	has appendectomy and is warned that his kidneys are deteriorating; *John Barleycorn*; his newly constructed

mansion, Wolf House, is destroyed by fire, a suspected arson

1914–15 travels to Mexico to report on the Revolution; returns to Hawaii for health, suffering from rheumatism and kidney disease

November 22, 1916 dies at Glen Ellen of gastrointestinal uremia and possibly self-induced drug overdose

Further Reading

London's Works
The Call of the Wild (Chicago: Nelson-Hall, 1980). London's most popular novel. This edition includes biographical sources, reviews, critical essays and a bibliography.

The Sea Wolf (New York: Macmillan, 1975).

Jack London: Short Stories, edited and with an introduction by Maxwell Geismar (New York: Hill and Lang, 1960). Good sampling of London's short fiction; selections range from the famous "To Build a Fire" to the more obscure, to the popular South Sea stories. Part of the American Century series.

Books About London
Ruth Franchere, *Jack London—The Pursuit of a Dream* (New York: Thomas Y. Crowell, 1962). Colorfully written biography, indexed and with a bibliography.

James Lundquist, *Jack London: Adventures, Ideas and Fiction* (New York: Ungar, 1987). Biographical portrait and critical study of the life and works of Jack London; covers a wide variety of the early stories, major novels and South Sea tales.

Irving Stone, *Jack London, Sailor on Horseback* (New York: Doubleday & Company, 1938). Popular and well-researched biographical novel on London's life.

Sherwood Anderson
(1876–1941)

*Sherwood Anderson—whom William Faulkner
called the "father of my generation of American
authors"—suffered a mid-life crisis and left
behind his family and career as a successful
businessman to become a writer.*
(Library of Congress)

*O*n a gray November day in 1912, a businessman from Elyria,
Ohio, was dictating a letter to his secretary when he suddenly
turned to her and said, "My feet are cold and wet. I have been
walking too long on the bed of a river."

With that odd and inexplicable statement, he stood up and left the office, never to return. Four days later he showed up in a drugstore in Cleveland, unshaven and still wearing his business clothes, which were now wrinkled and splattered with mud. He was dazed, confused and appeared to be suffering from amnesia. Clinging desperately to his last shred of sanity, he handed his address book to the druggist, hoping the man would be able to call a friend to come to his assistance.

The shocked druggist recognized the man. Why, it was Mr. Sherwood Anderson, the gentleman who used to run a mail-order business in Cleveland. The druggist shook his head and called one of Anderson's old business associates, who came down to collect him.

By leaving his office that day, Anderson walked out of obscurity and into American literary history. Caught up in a cultural revolution that challenged the conventions of the age, he soon became one of its leaders, profoundly influencing a generation of American writers who followed him, such as Ernest Hemingway, William Faulkner and F. Scott Fitzgerald.

The man who would have such a profound effect on American letters was born on September 13, 1876, in the small town of Camden, Ohio, the third of six children of Irwin and Emma (Smith) Anderson. The Andersons moved frequently so that Irwin could find work, and the family lived in a number of small Ohio towns before finally settling in Clyde. Anderson would later blend his imagined memories of Camden—the "little white town in a valley with high hills on each side," where the simple townspeople worked the fields by day and closeted themselves in their "poor little houses" at night—with his actual experiences in Clyde to write his most famous book, *Winesburg, Ohio* (1919).

The Andersons were one of the poorest families in Clyde, and young Sherwood helped out by taking on dozens of odd jobs around town. He was such a go-getter that people in Clyde nicknamed him "Jobby." Since "Jobby" Anderson was so busy working, his attendance in grammar school was erratic, and at 17 he quit high school, after attending for a total of only nine months. He went to work in a livery stable and then a bicycle factory in order to help support his family.

During his adolescence, Anderson experienced the usual anxieties and confusion about sex and his own sexuality, and the frustrations and mysteries of sexual desire became one of the themes of his fiction.

17

Reacting to the pressures of his unhappy home life, and because he was teased by other boys in the neighborhood, Anderson sometimes lapsed into momentary trances. In these states he saw his life "flying away" from him until it became a "speck in the distance" before returning to him "with a rush." In his biography, *Sherwood Anderson*, author Kim Townsend attributes these so-called "mystic episodes" to a psychological state of mind called a "fugue." Sometimes experienced in adolescence, a fugue is a condition in which the mind temporarily shuts out reality. Epilepsy is another possible explanation for Anderson's trances.

In 1895, Anderson's mother Emma died. His father abandoned the family, and suddenly there was nothing left in Clyde for the 19-year-old Sherwood. Like thousands of other midwesterners, he migrated to the big city of Chicago in 1896 to seek his fortune. He got work as a laborer and took accounting classes at night to advance his career.

After briefly serving in the military during the Spanish-American War, Anderson returned to Ohio in April of 1899 and enrolled in a high school equivalency course at Wittenberg College in Springfield. He befriended a local high school teacher who introduced him to what he called "fine literature."

Although he did well enough to earn entry to the college at Wittenberg, Anderson instead took a job offer from the advertising department of the *Woman's Home Companion* in Chicago. He became good at producing ad copy and by 1902 was writing articles for *Agricultural Advertising*, a trade journal.

"[A]dvertising gave [Anderson] the chance to write, and in writing the chance to come to terms with the conflicts in his life," Townsend observes. It may be hard to imagine that writing about canned peas could inspire such resolution of conflicts, yet it was the creativity and the daily practice at writing that cultivated Anderson's talent for loftier prose.

In 1903, Anderson met Cornelia Platt Lane, the daughter of a well-to-do president of a wholesale firm in Toledo, Ohio. She and Anderson courted for a year and married in the spring. Life was becoming more stable and prosperous for Anderson who turned 30 in 1906. He took charge of a Cleveland mail-order house while continuing to write business articles for trade publications. He managed the Cleveland company poorly, then struck out on his own in 1907 and founded the Anderson Manufacturing Company (later the American Merchants Company), a mail-order paint firm in Elyria, Ohio. That year his first son, Robert, was born; a year later another son, John, came along and in 1911 the Andersons had a daughter, Marion.

Although Anderson looked the part of the fine, upstanding member of the community, he sometimes became withdrawn, moody and self-absorbed. He often sought isolation in the sparsely furnished upstairs room in his house where he went to write.

He was obsessive about keeping the room spotlessly clean. In his own peculiar way, Anderson was attempting to cleanse himself and his environment of his social image. He had written for others long enough; now, he wanted to write for himself.

"I had become a writer," he recalled in *A Story Teller's Story* (1924). "Flinging aside the fake devotion that must always be characteristic of all such jobs as the advertising writing I had been doing for several years I had accepted my passion for scribbling."

And so he began to write the drafts of his first two novels, *Windy McPherson's Son* (1916), the story of a country boy's moral education in the big city of Chicago, and *Marching Men* (1917), an ode to labor leadership and the struggle of the working class in America. Neither book is representative of Anderson's best work, but each laid down a section of the foundation on which he would construct his masterpiece, *Winesburg, Ohio*.

In the winter of 1913, he left Cornelia and went to Chicago. The couple attempted several reunions, but it became evident to both of them that their marriage was no longer working. Anderson's leaving was actually something of a relief to Cornelia, since she was convinced that he was mentally unstable.

Meanwhile, Anderson took a job at the advertising firm of Taylor-Critchfield, continued to write fiction in his free time and began to associate with a local colony of artists, poets and writers. This group— the flower of the city's "literary renaissance"— included Floyd Dell, editor of the Chicago *Evening Post*'s "Friday Literary Review"; the quick-witted journalist, novelist and playwright Ben Hecht; and poet Carl Sandburg, who immortalized Chicago in his free verse as the "City of the Big Shoulders" and "Hog Butcher for the World."

This cultured crowd often met at Floyd Dell's apartment to tell stories, discuss art and shrug off the confines of conventionalism. Anderson longed to be one of them, and the moment he set foot in Floyd Dell's studio apartment he knew he was in the right place.

"A new life began for me," Anderson recalled in his *Memoirs* (1942). "It was a time of excitement, something seemingly new and fresh in the air we breathed."

State Street, Chicago, 1906. In the early 20th century, the city was emerging as both a commercial and cultural hub for the Midwest. Anderson— like many other midwesterners—came here to start a new life. He became a prominent member of the city's literary circle, which included poet Carl Sandburg.
(Library of Congress)

Here in Floyd Dell's apartment Anderson found an audience for his fiction. The group was impressed with *Windy McPherson's Son*, and Dell thought enough of the manuscript to place it in the hands of John Lane, a publisher in London, England. To Anderson's delight, Lane agreed to publish the book through the company's American branch.

Meanwhile, Anderson devoted more time to writing short fiction, the genre on which his reputation rests. The colorful collection of tenants in the ramshackle boarding house in which he lived provided inspiration for many of his characters.

"The idea I had was to take them, just as they were, as I felt them," Anderson wrote in his memoirs, "and transfer them from the city rooming house to an imagined small town . . ."

In turning his focus to small-town America, he was probably influenced by poet Edgar Lee Masters' *Spoon River Anthology* and

Hamlin Garland's *Main-Traveled Roads*, both of which took critical looks at life in the rural Midwest. But the town of Anderson's imagination—Winesburg, Ohio—and the characters who inhabited it were all his own, and the collection of stories that bears its name remains one of the most important works of American literature.

Winesburg, Ohio contains 23 short stories, most of which are woven together as the memories of George Willard, a writer and former reporter for the *Winesburg Eagle*. Each chapter is a fictional portrait of a member of the community. It was a narrative structure that Anderson credited himself with inventing. Each story is able to stand on its own, but the book's true craft and impact are appreciated most when the stories are read as a whole.

The stories first appeared between 1915 and 1916, published separately in periodicals like the *Masses*, a socialist publication edited by Floyd Dell, and *Seven Arts*, a new literary magazine in New York. *Winesburg, Ohio* as a collection would not find a publisher until 1919.

What makes *Winesburg, Ohio* such a powerful piece of literature is that the seemingly simple country people of Anderson's fictional town are not quite so simple. On the surface, they all play the assigned roles that one would expect to find in a small town—doctor, minister, school teacher. Yet inside they are desperate, tortured individuals, burdened with feelings of isolation, loneliness and defeat.

"Nothing ever turn[s] out" for the people of Winesburg, no more than for Enoch Robinson in the story "Loneliness":

> *He never grew up and of course he couldn't understand people and he couldn't make people understand him. The child in him kept bumping against things, against actualities like money and sex and opinions. Once he was hit by a streetcar and thrown against an iron post. That made him lame. It was one of the many things that kept things from turning out for Enoch Robinson.*

Enoch Robinson's deformity is more than physical: it is spiritual. As an old man, he tells George Willard the story of his thwarted career, his failed marriage and self-alienation. As Willard leaves, he hears the pathetic voice of the old man "whimpering . . . 'I'm all alone, all alone here . . .' "

Enoch Robinson and the other residents of Winesburg, Ohio, are indeed "all alone." They are cut off from each other and from society by fatal flaws in their natures.

Teacher Wing Biddlebaum in "Hands," for example, is at first admired for the quickness of his hands at strawberry-picking time. Wing's hands and how he touches people are his means of communicating approval, joy, affection. But when the imagination of "a half-witted boy" ignites a series of sexual abuse charges against him, he becomes an outcast and is forced to live on the edge of town.

The people of Winesburg exist in a rural wasteland that is in a state of decay and under the threat of extermination by the industrial age. The stern morality and Puritan values their forebears carried with them across the wilderness have crumbled and left them vulnerable and struggling. We can see evidence of this conflict in the story "The Strength of God," as the Reverend Curtis Hartman grapples with the "carnal desire to 'peep' " from behind the stained-glass window of the church tower into the bedroom of the school teacher, Kate Swift.

Anderson called these characters "grotesques," and defined them as people who "snatched up" truths for themselves and tried to live by them, only to find that they had become "falsehood." One after another, these grotesques seek out and confess to George Willard their innermost secrets in a final, desperate attempt to escape the imprisonment of their isolation. What Willard comes to realize is that liberation is possible only through compassion. He has compassion for these characters, but they cannot muster any for each other, and so they are doomed. In essence, *Winesburg, Ohio* is the story of one man's education through his exposure to the tragic experiences of others—"a background on which to paint the dreams of his manhood."

Winesburg, Ohio succeeds on different levels. On the one hand, it works as a classic book of American folk tales, illustrative of a way of life that has vanished. But *Winesburg, Ohio* is more significant for the way in which it challenged the literary standards and traditions of the day. The characters in *Winesburg, Ohio* are disturbing, not heroic; they are conflicted and complicated, not flat and identifiable. Anderson's straightforwardness on sexual issues shocked many readers, and he was compared to D. H. Lawrence, a British writer contemporary with Anderson whose books were condemned and sometimes banned for their eroticism.

But models for *Winesburg, Ohio* could be found closer to home. In his unconventional use of language and frank handling of human sexuality, Anderson was following in the footsteps of poet Walt Whitman. Like Mark Twain, he attacked and ridiculed the conventions of society. By stressing that fulfillment comes from within and that change is an essential element of human progress, he was resonating the philosophies of Ralph Waldo Emerson and Henry David Thoreau.

"The mass of men lead lives of quiet desperation," Thoreau had written. Anderson showed us, in intimate detail, who these people were.

In 1916, Anderson ended a two-year affair with Marietta "Bab" Finely, a reader at a local publishing company, and took up with a flamboyant and colorful sculptress and member of Floyd Dell's artistic colony, Tennessee Mitchell. She and Anderson joined a band of fellow artists that summer on a retreat to Lake Chateaugay in upstate New York, 30 miles north of Lake Placid, and not far from the Canadian border. By this time Cornelia had divorced Anderson, and so he was free to marry Mitchell in the little village of Chateaugay in July 1916.

In October, *Windy McPherson's Son* was published to mostly good reviews. The novel was compared to Twain's *The Adventures of Huckleberry Finn*, and Anderson was crowned the successor to Theodore Dreiser for his insights into the human condition, especially within the sweeping context of modern American urban life. Reviewer Waldo Frank in *Seven Arts* wrote that Anderson's first effort had "an unleashed and unsophisticated power that we have all along awaited in the American novel." At 40 years of age, Anderson had finally arrived.

By 1918, Anderson was working less on his advertising accounts at Taylor-Critchfield and more on his fiction and poetry. He produced a volume of 49 poems, *Mid-American Chants* (1918), which praised America's rural and agricultural tradition in the face of the modern era of industrialization. He also reworked the draft of his second novel, *Marching Men*, which turned out to be a failure. He himself admitted it "should have been an epic poem" instead of a novel.

Not to be discouraged, Anderson took a leave from Taylor-Critchfield, moved to New York City and began working on a new book. In just a few months he produced *Poor White* (1920), considered by many to be his best novel.

Drawn from childhood experiences, Anderson's story concerns the fictional town of Bidwell, Ohio. Part Winesburg, part Clyde, Bidwell is a simple midwestern town overrun by the complexities of the industrial age:

. . . all over the country, in the towns, the farm houses, and the growing cities of the new country, people stirred and awakened. Thought and poetry died or passed as a heritage to feeble fawning men who also became servants of the new order. Serious young men in Bidwell and other American towns, whose fathers had walked together on moonlit nights along Turner's Pike to talk of God, went away to technical schools.

Poor White has three main characters: Hugh McVey, his wife Clara Butterworth and the town of Bidwell itself.

McVey bears an unmistakable resemblance to Twain's Huck Finn. He is an idle dreamer, "born in a little hole of a town on a mud bank . . . on the Mississippi River," with a shiftless drunk for a father and a stern, practical Yankee "Aunt Polly" figure who later takes him under her wing. "[T]all, gaunt, [and] slow-speaking," McVey also bears a resemblance to Abraham Lincoln. Huck and Lincoln, in Anderson's estimation, were classic midwesterners.

Clara Butterworth is a so-called "modern woman" who struggles against the oppression of a late-Victorian, male-dominated society and thereby contributes to McVey's spiritual growth.

Finally, the town of Bidwell experiences its own growth through the gradual process of evolving from an agrarian community into a modern, midwestern city: "Men worked hard, but were much in the open air and had time to think. Their minds reached out toward the solution of the mystery of existence . . . There was a feeling, ill-expressed, that America had something real and spiritual to offer the rest of the world."

McVey, an inventor, is associated with the machinery and the gadgetry of the 20th century. He is seen by the men of Bidwell as the "instrument" of this "new forward-pushing impulse in American life." By inventing a cabbage-harvesting machine, he unwittingly sets off the spark of modernization in Bidwell. In doing so, he contributes to the destruction of his own environment and its loss of simple innocence.

In May 1919, Anderson's collection of stories about Winesburg was published. The reviews were good and Anderson began to earn his reputation as the spokesman for the new American Midwest. He followed up *Winesburg, Ohio* and *Poor White* with another collection of short stories, *The Triumph of the Egg* (1921), which included one of his most famous short stories, "The Egg."

Set in Bidwell, "The Egg" is the story of a chicken farmer who himself resembles an egg, with a "bald path over the top of his head" and a fat, round body. Like many of Anderson's "grotesques," the farmer is constantly victimized by his environment. "One unversed in such things can have no notion of the many and tragic things that can happen to a chicken," relates the farmer's son as he recalls his father's frustrated attempts to ward off the numerous poultry diseases and pitfalls that go along with the business. Among these are the various two-headed, five-legged "little monstrous things" that sometimes hatch from eggs, which the farmer preserves in jars of alcohol, believing them to be potential money-making attractions.

He brings them along and displays them in the restaurant that he opens after finally giving up on chicken farming. He is convinced that the way to bring in customers is to provide them with entertainment, such as showing them the deformed chickens, telling stories and performing a variety of tricks involving eggs.

He is about as successful at entertainment, however, as he was at chicken farming, and the ultimate "triumph of the egg" takes place when he absurdly tries to pass one through the neck of a bottle. Defeated, he reverently places an egg on the table before his wife, then kneels at her feet and weeps, leaving his son with the terrible legacy of wondering "why eggs had to be and why from the egg came the hen who again laid the egg."

The egg is an obvious symbol of life. It is mysterious, unyielding, simple in appearance yet complex in nature, and extremely fragile. The father's frustration thus stems from his inability to deal with life. He is "at once comical and pathetic," as Anderson scholar Rex Burbank observed—a classic example of the "grotesque" character who haunts Anderson's fiction, trying desperately to manipulate a world he cannot even begin to understand.

Anderson worked on this story and others, plus the draft of his next novel, *Many Marriages* (1923), in Mobile, Alabama, where he spent the winter and spring of 1920. Back in Illinois, he continued to work sporadically at Taylor-Critchfield and moved to the suburbs. When *Poor White* came out, his work was spoken of in the same breath as F. Scott Fitzgerald's *This Side of Paradise* and Sinclair Lewis's *Main Street*.

One evening in January of 1921, he attended a party at a coworker's apartment and there met a scruffy and struggling young writer named Ernest Hemingway, who had recently arrived in Chicago.

Like legions of other aspiring young writers of the day who went about with dog-eared copies of *Winesburg, Ohio* stuffed into their pockets, Hemingway looked up to the older, established author. Anderson became Hemingway's mentor and later brought his work to the attention of publisher Horace Liveright, of Boni & Liveright.

(Hemingway eventually repaid Anderson's generosity by writing *Torrents of Spring*, a scathing parody of Anderson's 1925 novel *Dark Laughter*. Anderson was puzzled and hurt by this unwarranted attack.)

In May of 1921 Anderson went to Paris where he was welcomed into Gertrude Stein's celebrated circle of literary disciples. There he met such contemporary writers as James Joyce, Ezra Pound, T. S. Eliot, Ford Maddox Ford and John Dos Passos.

When he returned to the United States four months later, his *Triumph of the Egg* was being hailed by the critics for its "glamorous beauty" and "unmistakable power." He was given the first *Dial* award (for a contribution to literature by "a young American writer") by the editors of *The Dial*. *The Dial* was a highly respected literary magazine founded by the Transcendentalists, a 19th-century group of American writers and philosophers, based largely in New England, who believed that the natural world was a unified reflection of spiritual truths and that the path to enlightenment could be found by seeking out these basic truths. (See *Nineteenth-Century Writers* by Steven Otfinoski, an "American Profiles" book published by Facts On File for more information on Transcendentalism.)

The *Dial* award included a cash prize of $2,000, which gave Anderson the means and the courage to finally quit his job at Taylor-Critchfield and go to New Orleans for the winter of 1922. He lived a comfortable life there, taking in the colorful and curious sights of the city and writing stories for the *Double Dealer*, a local literary magazine that also published the works of Hemingway, Faulkner and Hart Crane.

Anderson's next novel, *Many Marriages*, was widely considered to be a colossal failure. But Anderson redeemed himself with *Horses and Men* (1923), another collection of short stories, which included a number of his greatest tales, such as "The Man Who Became a Woman," "I Want to Know Why" and "I'm a Fool." *Horses and Men* and *The Triumph of the Egg* represent "the heights of [Anderson's] genius" as a short story writer, according to Rex Burbank; rarely did he ever approach this level of craft and quality again.

By now Anderson had once again fallen in love with another woman, this time a bookstore manager in New York named Elizabeth Prall. His relationship with Tennessee Mitchell had always been somewhat detached (the two only occasionally lived together and maintained separate residences throughout their marriage). In 1924 he moved to Reno, Nevada, where divorces could be easily had after a six-month residency. He spent his time in Reno working on his first autobiography, *A Story Teller's Story*, and married Prall as soon as his divorce came through.

The couple moved to New Orleans where Anderson met Horace Liveright, the dashing and colorful New York publisher, of Boni & Liveright. Anderson was in the market for a new publisher and Liveright agreed to take him on. While in New Orleans, Anderson also met William Faulkner. Like Hemingway, Faulkner initially revered Anderson but later took some shots at his former mentor in reviewing *Many Marriages* and *A Story Teller's Story*. Perhaps out of regret, Faulkner finally acknowledged his respect for Anderson in a posthumous 1953 tribute, "Sherwood Anderson: An Appreciation," in which he called Anderson "a giant in an earth populated to a great . . . extent by pygmies."

In 1925, Boni & Liveright published Anderson's one best-selling novel, *Dark Laughter*, which was inspired by Anderson's exposure to the lives of Southern blacks. Although the book was a popular success, it was taken to task by many of Anderson's contemporaries for its meandering style. Fitzgerald simply called it "lousy," and Hemingway found rich material for his parody in Anderson's stylistic habit of asking the reader questions in the narrative.

Anderson pressed on, however, and published another autobiography, *Tar: A Midwest Childhood*, and *Sherwood Anderson's Notebook*, a compilation of previously published pieces together with some new sketches (both 1926). During 1926 and 1927, he went out on the lecture circuit to raise some badly needed capital. He had purchased a farm in Marion, Virginia, and was building a large country home there, which he christened Ripshin, after a creek that ran through the property.

He also bought two competing local newspapers—the *Smythe County News* and the *Marion Democrat*—and fancied himself a country publisher. The people in the small town of Marion, however, resented a big-time writer barging into their lives and editorializing on their community affairs. Anderson eventually grew tired of the whole business and turned over the reins to his eldest son, Robert. He published some of his sketches from the papers in *Hello Towns!* (1929).

By the late 1920s, Anderson had lost his edge as a writer, and the reviewers claimed that he was "dying before our eyes." This type of criticism threw Anderson into moods of suicidal depression, and his mood wasn't elevated any by the failure of his third marriage. Yet Anderson, as Kim Townsend observed, "was a man who constantly renewed, remade himself." At 54 years of age he found a new companion (Eleanor Copenhaver, a society girl from a distinguished Marion family) and a new cause—politics.

Revitalizing a theme he had touched on in *Marching Men*, he became passionately dedicated to improving the lot of the working class in America. He spoke at rallies in the South, lobbied on behalf of workers' rights before labor organizations in New York, and went to Washington, D.C., to personally deliver a letter of protest to President Herbert Hoover. Anderson summed up his stance on the unfair treatment of the working class in his novel *Beyond Desire* (1932), which ends with a violent clash between striking workers and National Guard troops.

In 1933, Anderson published his final book of short stories, *Death in the Woods and Other Stories*, and married Eleanor Copenhaver. She made him happier than any of his previous wives, and he was beginning to feel more at peace. Just as John Steinbeck was to do a few years later, Anderson went on the road in 1934, gathering material for a series of articles about the poverty-stricken towns of the Midwest and the people there who had been crippled by the Great Depression. He collected many of these articles in *Puzzled America* (1935). His last novel, a romance named *Kit Brandon*, was published the following year.

Anderson enjoyed a minor revival during the late thirties. *Winesburg, Ohio* and stories from *The Triumph of the Egg* were produced as popular stage productions. In 1937, he was elected to the National Institute of Arts and Letters. During these years his byline could be found in numerous periodicals, including *The New Republic*, the *Nation* and various socialist-movement publications.

He maintained his interest in politics until his very last days. He was cruising toward the Panama Canal on a goodwill tour of South America in February of 1941 when he was struck with peritonitis, brought on by a perforated intestine. He hung on for three days until the ship came into port. He was rushed to the hospital at Colón in the Canal Zone and died there on March 8.

Today, Anderson may seem too old-fashioned for the modern reader. Indeed, many of his longer works are heavily draped in symbolism and ramble on about this or that cause, such as truth and the struggle for justice, in ways that are not always effective.

But, on closer inspection, we find much in Anderson that has relevance today. The influence of technology on traditional moral behavior, the effect of industrialism on the environment, the strained relationships that can exist between men and women, between human beings and their social institutions—these are all themes that can be found in the pages of Anderson's fiction and in the daily events of our own lives.

Above all, Anderson helped to bring the modern American short story into existence. He refined and advanced the literary technique of character development through the use of introspection and self-exploration—threads of technique he had picked up from Whitman and Stephen Crane. He allowed us to observe the way simple, ordinary people react when faced with "intense moments of happiness, defeat, triumph or revelation," as critic Rex Burbank puts it. We watch as they "move from the moral certainty of youth to the difficult adult world of ambiguities and paradoxes."

William Faulkner once called Anderson "the father of my generation of American writers," and he was right. Faulkner, Hemingway, Fitzgerald, Steinbeck, Wolfe, Dos Passos—all were influenced by the pioneering achievements of Sherwood Anderson. And if he was the father of Faulkner's generation, he could be considered the grandfather of this one, as we can trace his literary bloodline through the works of John Cheever, Flannery O'Connor, Raymond Carver, John Updike and others.

In a letter to a friend, Anderson wrote that "man's real life is lived out there in the imaginative world," and that it was a writer's obligation to seek reality out there. Anderson spent a lifetime wandering up and down the streets of his "imaginative world"— the world of *Winesburg, Ohio*, of Bidwell and other prototypical American towns that still exist today.

What he showed us was that there were things we may not always like to see or learn about ourselves, but to which we must necessarily turn every time we examine our heritage and question how far we as a moral nation have come.

Chronology

September 13, 1876	born in Camden, Ohio
1900	graduates high school and gets work writing advertising copy in Chicago
1913	leaves family life behind to become a writer after suffering nervous breakdown; first short story "The Rabbit Pen" published the following year
1916	*Windy McPherson's Son*, first novel
1919	*Winesburg, Ohio*
1921	*The Triumph of the Egg*; meets Hemingway; travels to Paris, meets Gertrude Stein and others
1923	*Horses and Men*; divorces second wife, marries third; travels to New Orleans following year and meets Faulkner
1927	buys farm and builds home in Marion, Virginia; buys two local newspapers
1930	meets woman who will be his fourth wife; becomes politically active
1933	*Death in the Woods and Other Stories*
March 8, 1941	dies of peritonitis in the Panama Canal Zone while on goodwill trip sponsored by the U.S. State Department

Further Reading

Anderson's Works

Winesburg, Ohio, edited by John H. Ferres (New York: Viking Press, 1966). This Viking Critical Library edition offers a variety of critical views of the book together with relevant selections from Anderson's memoirs.

The Portable Sherwood Anderson, edited with introduction by Horace Gregory (New York: Viking Press, 1949). Good sampling of Anderson's stories, essays, plus excerpts from novels.

Sherwood Anderson's Memoirs, A Critical Edition, edited by Ray Lewis White (Chapel Hill: University of North Carolina Press, 1969). Substantial autobiography, of particular help to the student doing in-depth work on Anderson and his life.

Books About Anderson

Kim Townsend, *Sherwood Anderson* (Boston: Houghton Mifflin, 1987). An adult biography that provides a good overview of Anderson's life and works.

Ray Lewis White, editor, *The Achievement of Sherwood Anderson, Essays in Criticism* (Chapel Hill: University of North Carolina Press, 1966). A variety of critical views of Anderson's works by his contemporaries and later scholars.

Willa Cather
(1876–1947)

Willa Cather in New York in 1912, the year her first novel, Alexander Bridge, *was published. The former Nebraska farmgirl had just left her job as managing editor of* McClure's Magazine—*a rare position of power for a woman in those days—and was on her way to becoming one of the greatest novelists of her time.*
(Willa Cather Pioneer Memorial Collection, Nebraska State Historical Society)

*T*he same year that Sherwood Anderson was writing stories about the citizens of "Winesburg," Ohio, another writer from the Midwest had just made a name for herself with her second novel. Like Anderson, hers was the story of a small-town, agrarian community existing on the fringes of modern society; like Anderson, she had lovingly drawn her settings and characters from her memories of a rural childhood.

Yet unlike Anderson, whose characters are grotesquely detached from the land and each other, the players in her drama share a common connection with the vast, open prairies and the "miles of fresh-plowed soil . . . [h]eavy and black, full of strength and harshness."

The author's name was Willa Cather, and the publication of her 1913 novel *O Pioneers!* was significant in American literature, since the book was one of the first serious, artistic attempts to portray the taming and settlement of the American West.

The author of *O Pioneers!* was something of a pioneer and a trailblazer herself. Her novel was one of the first books in American literature to focus on the lives of an immigrant class of people, in this case the Swedes, and Cather was one of the first great feminist writers of the century—prefiguring writers such as Eudora Welty, Flannery O'Connor, Muriel Spark, Doris Lessing or Margaret Atwood—to hold her own in the male-dominated world of American letters.

Willa Sibert Cather was born on December 7, 1873, in Back Creek, Virginia, the eldest of seven children of Charles and Mary Boak Cather. Women played a significant role in inspiring Cather in early life. Her maternal grandmother, Rachel Boak, was a model of self-reliance. Widowed at 38, she reared five children on her own and had a hand in raising young Willa at Willow Shade, the Cathers' family homestead. Another important influence was Mary Ann Anderson, a mountain woman who often visited the Cathers and kept Willa captivated for hours with stories of her backwoods neighbors high in the Blue Ridge Mountains.

Grandma Boak and Mary Ann Anderson would later appear in Cather's fiction as Rachel Blake and Mrs. Ringer in *Sapphira and the Slave Girl* (1940), Cather's ode to her family history and her only novel of the South.

Cather continued to feel a close bond with women throughout her life, and it is now generally assumed among critics that she was a lesbian. As a girl she preferred to wear her hair cut short and was called a "tomboy." In her adult life she had several affairs with and romantic attachments to women and lived with Edith Lewis, her friend and companion for almost 40 years. Homosexuality in those days was not openly discussed, and Cather took considerable efforts—such as burning all her correspondence— to conceal the details of her personal life.

Life changed for the young Willa in 1883 when Charles Cather decided to yank his family's roots from the ancestral Virginian sod and replant them in the wilds of Nebraska. Separation from the gentle, pastoral setting of Willow Shade was hard on the nine-year-old Willa, and, as Phyllis C. Robinson points out in Willa, *The Life of Willa Cather*, "change and loss . . . followed Willa Cather all her life . . . and in time became the themes that dominate her fiction."

Cather's new Nebraska home was in the very middle of the continental United States, in a vast open swath of plain and prairie between the Little Blue and Republican rivers, known as the Divide.

"There seemed to be nothing to see," Cather's alter ego, Jim Burden, recalls in Cather's autobiographical novel, *My Ántonia* (1918). "[N]o fences, no creeks or trees, no hills or fields . . . There was nothing but land: not a country at all, but the material out of which countries are made."

The people here were different as well. For the first time in her life, Cather set eyes on Germans, Scandinavians, Poles, Czechs, Bohemians and a host of other European peoples, all lured there by the same promise of land that had attracted Eastern farmers like Charles Cather.

As one might expect of a person destined to be a writer, Cather was a curious and investigative child. In no time at all she befriended her new neighbors and pressed them for stories, as she had with Mary Ann Anderson back in Virginia. She would later recall the dignity and courage of these immigrant peoples in the pages of her fiction.

The Cathers joined a small farming community of fellow Virginians, just northwest of the town of Red Cloud. Charles Cather quickly grew tired of farming, however, and moved his family once again, this time to Red Cloud where Willa first attended school.

Cather was a bright and interested student, and her good grades got her into the state university in Lincoln in 1891. There she began contributing stories and poetry to the campus literary publication. By her junior year, she was writing stories and dramatic reviews for the Lincoln newspaper, the *Journal*, under the editorial supervision of Will Owen Jones, who became a lifelong friend and mentor.

After graduation in 1895 she returned to Red Cloud, where she continued to write a column for the *Journal* and spent a listless year at home wondering what to do with her life. An answer came when she was offered the editorship of a new woman's magazine in Pittsburgh, the *Home Monthly*.

Cather happily accepted the job and left Nebraska, never to live there again. However, no matter how famous she became, she always returned in the summers. Her years on the Divide in Nebraska had had a lasting impact on her.

After a year at the *Home Monthly*, she left to write articles for various other publications, but always kept the dream of writing fiction in the back of her mind.

In 1899 she met Isabelle McClung, the daughter of a prominent judge. She became a regular guest at the McClung table

As a young tomboy in Nebraska, Cather liked to keep her hair cut short. She was born "Wilella" but changed her name to "Willa" to honor her maternal grandfather (a member of the Virginia legislature) and her uncle (a Civil War hero), both of whom were named William.
(Willa Cather Pioneer Memorial Collection, Nebraska State Historical Society)

and was accepted there as a surrogate daughter. She eventually moved in with the family and developed a lifelong romantic attachment to Isabelle.

In the summer of 1902, she visited Europe on assignment for the *Nebraska State Journal*. She despised England but fell in love with France and returned to Pittsburgh after four months, determined to make a living as a writer.

Her dream came true when she began selling her stories of life on the Divide to Eastern literary publications such as *Harper's Weekly* and *New England Magazine*. By 1903, she had collected enough of her poetry to publish a volume, *April Twilights*, which celebrated the sum of her experience to that point—home life on the plains and the splendors of Europe.

Cather was beginning to be noticed, and she had the good fortune to catch the career-making eye of S. S. McClure, founder of *McClure's Magazine*, publisher of Jack London and partner in the publishing house of McClure, Phillips. McClure, always on the lookout for new talent, summoned Cather to his New York office for an interview. When he learned that several of her manuscripts had been rejected by readers at his magazine, he called them in to reprimand them in front of Cather. Hinting that he had plans for her, McClure encouraged Cather to send him some more stories.

Back in Lincoln in 1903, Cather met Edith Lewis. Lewis would play an important part in Cather's life, serving as her faithful companion, friend, assistant and, in all likelihood, lover throughout most of the writer's career. Although Cather was obviously quite fond of Lewis, she remained romantically devoted to Isabelle McClung.

Cather's exposure to the sophistication of city living in contrast to her rustic life on the Divide set the tone for her first collection of short stories, *The Troll Garden* (1905), published by McClure. "The Sculptor's Funeral," "A Wagner Matinee" and "Paul's Case" (her most anthologized story and considered by critics to be one of the finest in the English language) are representative of the book's theme.

The sculptor Harvey Merrick, who escapes a dull-witted life of drudgery on a Nebraska farm to become a famous artist; the classically-trained musician Aunt Georgina, whose spirit withers on the empty plain for 30 years, only to be revived by a visit to a Boston concert hall; the disgruntled teacher Paul, who sacrifices everything he has for a few days of splendor on the streets of New York City—all these characters struggle with the conflicts that exist between their harsh, uncultured environments and the pursuit of art, beauty and refinement.

As scholar James Woodress observed, Cather made these juxtapositions throughout her career: East vs. West, experience vs. innocence, civilization vs. primitivism. These conflicts have their origin in Cather's lingering memories of her Virginia childhood contrasted with her Nebraska upbringing. They are later reinforced by the vast differences between her urban experiences and her isolated existence on the prairie. Cather remained poised between the two worlds, like Aunt Georgina who realized that waiting for her "just outside the door of the concert hall"—even as the last, powerful chords of the Wagnerian overture fade away—lay the more awesome and "inconceivable silence of the plains."

The Troll Garden won high praise from the critics and in 1906 McClure offered Cather a staff job on his magazine, where her short stories began to appear regularly. McClure was so pleased with Cather's work that he made her managing editor of the magazine, a rare opportunity for a woman in those days.

The job was exciting but draining. It left Cather little time to work on her fiction outside of trips to Europe, in search of new writers for the magazine, and summer visits to Red Cloud. She did manage to publish "The Enchanted Bluff" in April of 1909 in *Harper's Weekly*.

This nostalgic story about a group of boys telling tales around a campfire is pivotal in Cather's career because it represents a shift in her treatment of Nebraska. Whereas in *The Troll Garden* the prairie is depicted as an empty outpost of civilization, in "The Enchanted Bluff" Cather describes the land and the rivers she knew as a girl in loving detail. Here the "little willow seedlings emerged triumphantly from the yellow froth" of the river in springtime, the "cottonwood . . . glittered" and the "dancing willow wands" swayed beneath the moonlight.

In 1911, she began work on her first novel, *Alexander's Bridge* (1912), the story of an engineer from the West who comes to the East to build bridges. Bartley Alexander's life eventually collapses, like one of his bridges, when he is torn between faithfulness to his wife and his love for an actress with whom he has an affair.

By the fall of 1911, the strain of working on her book coupled with her responsibilities at the magazine became too much and Cather took a sabbatical in the hills of western New York state. Here she wrote the long story, "The Bohemian Girl," whose main character, Clara Vavrika Ericson, is the predecessor of Alexandra

Bergson, the powerful heroine of *O Pioneers!* It was one of Cather's first pieces written from a female rather than male point of view.

Cather didn't think that her story of Swedish and Bohemian settlers on the Divide would have mass appeal, but it turned out she was wrong. The popularity of "The Bohemian Girl," coupled with that of *Alexander's Bridge,* convinced her to retire from magazine editing and pursue writing full-time.

After a transformational trip to Arizona and New Mexico, where Cather's eyes were opened to the beauties of the desert, she and Edith Lewis settled back in New York in a new spacious apartment at Number 5 Bank Street.

Cather now resumed work on another novel she had begun on sabbatical. At times, her new book seemed to be about nothing but corn and cows, she told her friends. She feared that not more than a half a dozen people might be interested in reading it. Yet she also had great faith in the book and pressed on.

"[F]rom the first chapter, I decided not to 'write' at all," Cather told an interviewer in 1921, "[but] simply to give myself up to the pleasure of recapturing in memory people and places I had believed forgotten."

What she recaptured became *O Pioneers!,* the story of Alexandra Bergson's struggle to keep her Swedish immigrant family's farm going after the death of her father. Alone in her strength and abilities, surrounded by less capable persons who are of no help, Alexandra succeeds in building up the farm into a prosperous business, only to have her hopes for the future dashed when her young brother, Emil, is killed by a jealous husband. Alexandra comes to terms with the tragedy and marries Carl Linstrum to ease her loneliness. Her deep devotion to the land underlies the novel:

> *It seemed beautiful to her, rich and strong and glorious. Her eyes drank in the breadth of it, until her tears blinded her. The Genius of the Divide, the great, free spirit which breathes across it, must have bent lower than it ever bent to a human before. The history of every country begins in the heart of a man or woman.*

Alexandra Bergson is one of American literature's earliest heroines, following in the footsteps of Nathaniel Hawthorne's Hester Prynne and blazing the trail for such spirited and independent female characters as Ma Joad in John Steinbeck's *The Grapes of Wrath.*

Although "[t]here seemed to be nothing to see" out on Nebraska's Great Divide, Cather found plenty there to write about in her novels and short stories.
(Willa Cather Pioneer Memorial Collection, Nebraska State Historical Society)

O Pioneers! was a critical success and launched Cather's writing career. "[F]ar above the ordinary . . . touched with genius . . . American in the best sense of the word," were phrases reviewers used to describe it. To a reading public accustomed to a dainty diet of cultivated, upper-class characters and plots, Cather had served up a heaping plateful of true prairie grit and determination, and they ate it up.

Cather's next book, *The Song of the Lark* (1915), was inspired by profiles she wrote of three American opera singers, particularly the colorful Olive Fremsted.

On a second trip to the Southwest, in 1915, Cather visited Mesa Verde, the prehistoric home of a vanished tribe of cliff-dwelling Indians she had heard about. The ancient mysticism of the place intrigued her and had figured in her story "The Enchanted Bluff" and eventually in "Tom Outland's Story," a section of her novel *The Professor's House* (1925).

After receiving an honorary doctorate from the University of Nebraska in 1916, Cather found a new place to write in the foothills of New Hampshire's Mount Monadnock. The Shattuck Inn in the little village of Jaffrey became a retreat for her and Lewis over the years, and it was here that the author began to write her next novel, *My Ántonia*.

Inspired by memories stirred up during Cather's trips home to Red Cloud, *My Ántonia* is the story of Ántonia Shimerda, a pioneer girl forced to work as a servant after her father, unable to make it as a farmer, commits suicide. She runs off with a railway conductor, but returns to the Divide to marry Bohemian farmer Anton Cuzak and raise a family.

Cather conveys her story of life on the plains, and her impressions of the stouthearted men and women who carved out an existence there, through the eyes of narrator Jim Burden. The book is not so much about Ántonia Shimerda as it is about the mark she leaves on Burden. The tone and episodic pace of the book are governed by his recollections of Ántonia and of the cyclical pattern of life on the plains. There, people's livelihoods are inextricably linked to the change of seasons and to the stages of growth, death and renewal. "*My Ántonia* is, then, ultimately about time, about the inexorable movement of future into present, of present into past," scholar James E. Miller points out.

Burden sees Ántonia as one who is firmly anchored in this environment, a powerful symbol of human perseverance:

> *She was a battered woman now, not a lovely girl; but she still had that something which fires the imagination, could still stop one's breath for a moment by a look or gesture that somehow revealed the meaning in common things. She had only to stand in the orchard, to put her hand on a little crab tree and look up at the apples, to make you feel the goodness of planting and tending and harvesting at last . . . It was no wonder that her sons stood tall and straight. She was a rich mine of life, like the founders of early races.*

My Ántonia has been called a flawed novel by some scholars who have pointed out its various inconsistencies. Ántonia disappears from the narrative at times, and Cather introduces seemingly irrelevant characters and situations that never resurface. Yet *My Ántonia* was at the time, and still is, one of Cather's most popular novels.

Cather switched publishers in 1920 to join Alfred A. Knopf's growing stable of writers. Knopf published her next collection of short stories, *Youth and the Bright Medusa* (1920), which won Cather more critical acclaim. The praise climaxed in 1923 when she received the Pulitzer Prize for her newest novel, *One of Ours* (1922).

The hardy women of the Plains inspired such characters as Alexandra Bergson in O Pioneers! *and Ántonia Shimerda of* My Ántonia.
(Willa Cather Pioneer Memorial Collection, Nebraska State Historical Society)

The story of Claude Wheeler, a boy of the plains who dies on a World War I battlefield in France, *One of Ours* was based upon the true fate of one of Cather's cousins. Although the book was a best-seller and won the Pulitzer, there were those who accused Cather of romanticizing a serious world conflict. Cather stood by her novel, however, calling it her favorite despite what all "the high-brow critics" had to say about it.

Still, the critics had a point, which Cather herself was happy to admit. At almost 50 years of age, she belonged to a "backward" time. But this was because she found little to admire in the period of post–World War I expansionism that was changing the West she had known.

"[T]he world broke in two in 1922 or thereabout," she wrote. The Western states were being populated by a different breed of pioneer—industrialists and opportunists who bled the land, continued to abuse the rights of Native Americans and seemed to lack the moral fiber of early settlers in the territory. Cather's sentiments are summed up in this passage from *A Lost Lady* (1923), considered by many scholars to be her most beautifully crafted novel:

The Old West had been settled by dreamers, great-hearted adventurers who were unpractical to the point of magnificence; a courteous brotherhood, strong in attack but weak in defence, who could conquer but could not hold. Now all the vast territory they had won was to be at the mercy of men . . . who had never dared anything, never risked anything. They would drink up the mirage, dispel the morning freshness, root out the great brooding spirit of freedom, the generous, easy life of the great land-holders. The space, the colour, the princely carelessness of the pioneer they would destroy and cut up into profitable bits, as the match factory splinters the primeval forest.

Other works of this period that communicate Cather's mistrust of modernism are *The Professor's House* and *My Mortal Enemy* (1926).

A return visit to the Southwest in 1925 inspired her best-known novel, *Death Comes for the Archbishop* (1927). She was impressed with local stories about the courageous efforts of the early French missionaries in the territory. She based her novel of Bishop Jean Latour and his vicar, Father Joseph Vaillant, on the true story of two French clerics, Bishop Jean Baptiste Lamay and Father Joseph Machebeauf, who journeyed from a French village to establish a church in the American desert.

Death Comes for the Archbishop is notable for the loving friendship between Latour and Vaillant—no doubt inspired by Cather's long-standing relationship with Edith Lewis—and for its descriptions of the New Mexican landscape: "The air and the earth interpenetrated in the warm gusts of spring; the soil was full of sunlight, and the sunlight full of red dust. The air one breathed was saturated with earthy smells, and the grass under foot had a reflection of blue sky in it."

Cather achieves tension in the novel through her familiar use of contrast. She compares the pastoral life of the local Native Americans—a people living harmoniously with nature—with the aggressive commercialism of white society. The corrupted priests of the diocese, as well, are pitted against the purifying influence of Bishop Latour and his assistant, Vaillant.

"*Death Comes for the Archbishop*," recalled Edith Lewis in her 1953 memoir, *Willa Cather Living*, "was so unlike anything at all that was being written, the publishers were not prepared for its instant and overwhelming success . . ."

Book dealers had a difficult time keeping it on the shelves, and in no time at all, it achieved the rank of an American classic. It also "marked . . . the close of an era in Willa Cather's life," according to Edith Lewis. In the fall of 1927, the building she and Cather had lived in for 15 years was marked for demolition. A new subway was being built, and high-rise apartments were on the way. Again, modern times were catching up with Willa Cather.

The author was transient for a while, living in hotels and traveling abroad to Europe with Isabelle McClung as well as home to Red Cloud. A visit to the historic city of Quebec in 1928, coupled with a continuing interest in Catholicism, which had begun with *Death Comes for the Archbishop*, inspired her next work, *Shadows on the Rock* (1931). This historical novel of 18th-century Quebec was a tremendous commercial success and a Book-of-the-Month Club selection. The critics were less enthusiastic and labeled it a "dull" disappointment in the wake of *Death Comes for the Archbishop*.

The critics' jibes put no dent in Cather's reputation, however. She was awarded honorary degrees from Yale, Princeton, Smith and the University of California and was the distinguished guest lecturer at numerous academic gatherings. Her frank opinions on issues were usually colorful. Speaking before members of the Bowdoin College Institute of Modern Literature, she condemned the "modern novel, the motion picture and radio" as the three biggest "menace[s] to human culture."

The deaths of Cather's parents—her father in 1927 and her mother after a long illness in 1931—left her depressed and feeling cut off from her past and Red Cloud. She never returned to the little Nebraska town. Her sense of loss and loneliness was reflected in her melancholy novel, *Lucy Gayheart* (1935).

More deaths and tragedies befell Cather between 1935 and 1938. Her brother Douglass, with whom she was close, suffered a heart attack. A few months later she received news that Isabelle had died in Italy. On top of this, Cather was suffering from a wrist injury that made it excruciatingly painful for her to write (she handwrote her manuscripts), and she was forced to dictate all her correspondence. She couldn't possibly dictate her fiction, however, and endured agonizing pain while writing her final novel, *Sapphira and the Slave Girl*, a nostalgic rediscovery of her southern roots.

By the summer of 1941, Cather's health was declining. Recovering from gall bladder and appendix operations, she retreated in 1943 to Mt. Desert Island, Maine, where the azaleas were in bloom and the breezes were cool and mild. Back in New York she spent her final years receiving visitors and being nursed by Lewis.

On the morning of April 24, 1947, Lewis recalled that Cather was "never more herself . . . [h]er spirit was high, her grasp of reality as firm as always." But that afternoon the author had a massive cerebral hemorrhage and died alone in her room.

"Willa Cather and Nebraska grew up together," wrote scholar Alfred Kazin. So did the American West and the United States as a world power. Willa Cather observed this growth, took part in some of it and had something important to say about all that she saw.

Cather is sometimes passed over as simply a writer of pioneer stories. This is a mistake. She was also an insightful, sometimes harsh commentator on the decline of American values. She mourned what she perceived to be the loss of decency and simplicity in American society, so clearly enshrined, in her opinion, in the lives of the farmers and their families struggling to survive on the prairie.

Although today her name is not as exalted or familiar as Hemingway or Fitzgerald's, she nevertheless deserves credit for addressing the "defeat of a peculiarly American dream of innocence, grace [and] hope," in the words of scholar Harold Bloom. This was an achievement that predated Fitzgerald's attempt at such a thing in *The Great Gatsby* and occurred long before Hemingway would approach it in *For Whom the Bell Tolls*.

Chronology

December 7, 1873	born in Back Creek, Virginia
1883	moves with family to Nebraska
1895–96	graduates from University of Nebraska; takes job in Pittsburgh as editor of *Home Monthly*
1906	joins staff of *McClure's Magazine* in New York
1913	*O Pioneers!*
1918	*My Ántonia*
1923	wins Pulitzer Prize for *One of Ours*; publishes *A Lost Lady*
1927	*Death Comes for the Archbishop*
1940	*Sapphira and the Slave Girl*
April 24, 1947	dies in New York City

Further Reading

Cather's Works

O Pioneers! (New York: Penguin Books, 1989). This edition has an informative introductory essay and a bibliography.

Death Comes for the Archbishop (New York: Alfred A. Knopf, 1988). Handsome reissue of this classic.

Willa Cather: Early Novels and Short Stories (New York: Literary Classics of the United States, 1987). This excellent collection includes Cather's first book of fiction, *The Troll Garden*, plus the novels *The Song of the Lark, O Pioneers!, My Ántonia* and *One of Ours*; also provides extensive chronology. Part of the Library of America series.

Willa Cather in Person: Interviews, Speeches and Letters, selected and edited by L. Brent Bohlke (Lincoln: University of Nebraska Press, 1986). Provides insights into Cather's views on literature and the artistic life; an intimate look at this otherwise secretive author.

Books About Cather

Barbara Bonham, *Willa Cather* (Philadelphia: Chilton, 1970). Good, comprehensive and readable biography.

John J. Murphy, *My Ántonia: The Road Home* (Boston: Twayne, 1989). This exhaustive study of the novel offers a survey of criticism and a definitive bibliography. Part of Twayne's Masterworks Studies series.

F. Scott Fitzgerald
(1896–1940)

*The happy family—Scott and Zelda
Fitzgerald, and their only child, Scottie,
shown here at the height of Fitzgerald's
career in the early 1920s.*
(National Archives)

*I*t was a warm summer evening on the French Riviera. It was 1925,
a golden time of peace and prosperity between the first and second
world wars—a period in history that one bright and promising young
American author had already labeled "the Jazz Age."

This same American author now sat—drunk—at a private din-
ner party in the elegant villa of wealthy American friends. When
the dessert of pineapple sherbert and figs was placed before him,

he thought it would be amusing to pick up one of the figs and hurl it at the bare back of a French countess. Later, he took delight in tossing some expensive Italian goblets over a garden wall, just to hear the tinkling on the other side.

This troublemaker's name was F. Scott Fitzgerald. Despite his immature antics, he was one of the greatest writers of his generation—a generation he once described as having "grown up to find all Gods dead, all wars fought, all faiths in men shaken." He was the spokesman for this generation, and what he had to say reflected the events of his riotous and often sad life.

It was a life that began on September 24, 1896, in St. Paul, Minnesota. Francis Scott Key Fitzgerald was the third child of Edward and Mary (Molly) McQuinlan Fitzgerald. He could trace his paternal lineage from before the Revolutionary War and aristocratic roots in Maryland, to Francis Scott Key, the composer of "The Star Spangled Banner." He was proud of his heritage. He looked up to and admired his father, identifying in him all the gentility and manners of a Southern gentleman.

In 1898 Edward Fitzgerald's furniture business failed, and the frightened young Scott Fitzgerald prayed that the family wouldn't go to the poorhouse. The Fitzgeralds were rescued from this fate by Molly's wealthy mother, who invited them to move in with her.

The McQuinlan family fortune enabled young Scott to go to St. Paul Academy, a private high school in the city. At 11 years of age, Fitzgerald was a handsome youth with blond hair and striking green eyes. He was also bright and quick-witted.

He was not, however, very modest about these virtues and quickly developed a reputation as a show-off. On the athletic field, for example, if he couldn't be the pitcher or the quarterback, he didn't want to play.

Still, Fitzgerald could be great fun to be with. He had a devilish sense of humor and enjoyed pulling pranks. His attractiveness and humor also made him popular with the girls, and he was a flirt.

Fitzgerald's literary career began early. At St. Paul Academy, he was caught scribbling stories in class behind the cover of a large, propped-up geography book. Although he was a poor student, he exhibited a genuine love for reading and writing, and it was evident to his teachers that he knew how to tell a story.

He was encouraged to write by his headmaster and kept a journal, which he called the *Thoughtbook of Francis Scott Key Fitzgerald*. In it he recorded his romantic adventures—both real and imagined—and his dreams of being popular. He was also a habitual compiler of long lists, charts and tables of people and events. This compulsion no doubt contributed to his ability to arrange the details of a story into a narrative structure and thus to his development as a writer. His first published piece, "The Mystery of Raymond Mortgage," appeared in the school magazine in the fall of 1909. When the newly printed magazine arrived at school, Fitzgerald spent the day lingering in the hallways, counting the number of people he saw reading his story.

In 1911 Fitzgerald got a taste of what it was like to rub elbows with the privileged class when he went to the Newman School, an exclusive Catholic boarding school in New Jersey. It was the kind of thing he strove to do all his life. Never forgetting the panic he felt as a child when his father lost his job, Fitzgerald remained status-conscious and longed to go to an Ivy League school. He chose Princeton, which Amory Blaine, the hero of his first novel, *This Side of Paradise* (1920), describes as "lazy and good-looking and aristocratic . . . the pleasantest country club in America." Fitzgerald did poorly on his entrance exams, even though he cheated on them, and had to "bicker" his way into the school.

The Princeton of Fitzgerald's day, with its Gothic spires and ivy-covered buildings, was one of the three most prestigious universities in the country, the others being Harvard and Yale. Founded in 1746, the school had borrowed the "club" system from Oxford and Cambridge universities in England. The clubs—unique to Princeton—were like elite fraternities whose sole function was to provide social status to their members, and getting into the right one could make or break your college career.

Also essential, as far as Fitzgerald was concerned, was being on the football team. The role of the Big Man on Campus was a very important one for the socially conscious Scott Fitzgerald, as typified in the following passage from *This Side of Paradise*:

> *Now, far down the shadowy line of University Place, a white-clad phalanx broke the gloom, and marching figures, white-shirted, white-trousered, swung rhythmically up the street, with linked arms and heads thrown back [in song] . . . There at the head of the white platoon was Allenby, the football captain, slim and defiant, as if aware that this year the hopes of the college rested on him, that his hundred-and-sixty pounds were expected to dodge to victory through the heavy blue and crimson lines.*

Fitzgerald didn't get much of a chance to "dodge" through many lines at Princeton. He lasted three days on the freshman football squad and retired with an ankle injury. Realizing he had to make a name for himself in some other way, he directed his energies toward getting into the Triangle, a drama club, and to publishing stories in the school humor magazine, *The Tiger*.

After having some short pieces accepted by *The Tiger*, he wrote some longer, more serious stories for another school publication, the *Nassau Literary Magazine* (or just the *Lit*, as it was known on campus).

Fitzgerald's contributions to *The Tiger* were brief, unsigned jokes, parodies and poems. However, when he turned his hand to writing more serious literature for the pages of the *Lit*, what emerged were stories and one-act plays centered around his personal experiences, both past and present. He wrote of fathers who were failures, drawing on his childhood memories, and of uncertainties about his Catholic religion in the face of so much Protestantism. He also fictionalized his pursuit of, and admiration for, young women.

In addition to writing for campus publications, his college career included other, less acceptable extracurricular activities. He had taken up smoking and developed a strong taste for whiskey and champagne. He would go off on wild drinking binges with his college companions, sometimes missing days of classes. Naturally, his grades suffered and on more than one occasion the college officials warned him to watch his step.

By the first half of his junior year, Fitzgerald was flunking out and was told he would have to repeat the courses he had failed. He caught malaria (Princeton was located near bug-infested swamps) and withdrew in January of 1916 to take a break and get well. He stayed with his parents in St. Paul and returned to school in the fall. Since poor grades barred a student from holding positions of importance in the clubs, all hopes of a successful career at Princeton were dashed. But a war that had been raging in Europe since 1914 gave him one last shot, or so he thought, at making a hero of himself.

The United States entered World War I in 1917. Fitzgerald was called into the army and left Princeton for good, without receiving a diploma. He was sent to a training camp in Kansas, where it was cold, harsh and miserable compared to the life he had led in college. He killed time by scribbling away at a novel he called *The Romantic Egoist*. The story would later become *This Side of Paradise*, a novel about an ambitious, socially conscious young man's days at Princeton and his subsequent disappointments in life at having failed to meet his own expectations.

50

F. Scott Fitzgerald

In April of 1918, Fitzgerald's outfit was transferred to a camp near Montgomery, Alabama. In July of that year, at a country club dance, he met a girl by the name of Zelda Sayre. The daughter of a local judge and just a few weeks shy of 18, Zelda had honey-colored hair, blue eyes and a fragile, gracious figure. But beneath this southern belle's seemingly innocent exterior was an altogether different creature.

Named after a gypsy queen, Zelda was a lively, headstrong, spontaneous young woman who did whatever she wanted, which was usually something outrageous. If she was bored, no matter where she was, she would start dancing, just to amuse herself. She enjoyed riding in fast cars over bumpy roads, smoking cigarettes, drinking gin and driving her father crazy by sneaking out of her window at night to go to parties. She possessed an adventurous streak of willfulness and charm that made her most popular with the boys and feared by other girls.

It was this combination of sculptured beauty and wild, unpredictable behavior that hooked Fitzgerald from the first moment he laid eyes on her. They complemented each other's good looks and love of adventure. Moreover, Zelda's antics provided Fitzgerald with new material for his fiction. Sometimes copying, almost word for word, her off-handed expressions and her carefree attitude toward life, Fitzgerald used the raw material of Zelda's lively personality to create a specific type of character.

Rosalind in *This Side of Paradise*, Gloria in *The Beautiful and Damned* (1922) and Nicole in *Tender Is the Night* (1934) were all based on Zelda at different periods of her life. She was the "original American flapper," she once told a reporter—a light-hearted, fun-loving wisp of a girl at a tender age who dances through life as if it were one never-ending party, totally oblivious to its grim realities.

While Fitzgerald was awaiting his orders to go overseas, he spent much of his free time on the front porch of the Sayre house, wooing Zelda. In other spare moments, he continued to work on *The Romantic Egoist*, which he sent off to Scribner's in New York. It was sent back with suggestions for improvement. Fitzgerald made the revisions, but it was turned down a second time, even though one editor at Scribner's, Maxwell Perkins, was very impressed with the book. Perkins, who later edited Ernest Hemingway, Thomas Wolfe and other notable authors of the day, was to become Fitzgerald's editor and one of his closest friends.

The war ended in 1918, never giving Fitzgerald a chance to become a hero. He was forced to leave Alabama as well as Zelda, but he had already made up his mind to marry her. He had no job, however, and no income, so he went to New York and got work at an advertising agency writing streetcar sign ads at $90 a week. He continued to write fiction and sent off dozens of short stories to magazines, miserably accumulating rejection slips and drinking heavily. Unhappy at the ad firm, he finally quit his job and went home to St. Paul. He worked hard at revising *The Romantic Egoist*, which he retitled *This Side of Paradise*, and sent it off once again to Scribner's. This time it was accepted, and Fitzgerald was on his way to fame and fortune.

This Side of Paradise was an instant success, both commercially and critically. With the story of Amory Blaine, a snobbish young man who goes to Princeton, falls in and out of love and becomes disillusioned before his thirtieth birthday, the novel paralleled Fitzgerald's life practically to the letter. In this new book about a new era, written in a new way, Fitzgerald had captured the essence of his generation. Through his depictions of campus life—of girls as "flirts" and of "petting parties"—he told the story of America's new and daring youth, who were rejecting the dusty morals and restrictions of the Victorian era.

Though awkwardly structured, the book was topical and pegged to an exact and exciting moment in America that came to be known as "the Jazz Age" (thanks, in part, to Fitzgerald himself). It was an era of determined, reckless, happy abandon. World War I was over and America, experiencing a boom in the economy, also experienced a new sense of freedom, a relaxation of the stiff morality of the past. It was a time of dancing the "Charleston," of bobbed hair and short skirts for "flapper girls," and of staying out all night long in "speakeasies" which were illegal drinking establishments, since the United States had declared prohibition against alcohol in 1919. Fitzgerald, because of the life-style he adopted and the things he wrote about, became closely associated with the Jazz Age and was swept up in its powerful momentum.

The success of *This Side of Paradise* allowed Fitzgerald to marry Zelda, and the two of them spent a wild two-week honeymoon at the luxurious Biltmore Hotel in New York City before they were asked to leave because of their reckless behavior. They moved to a country home in Westport, Connecticut, where Fitzgerald worked on his next novel, *The Beautiful and Damned* (1922), while writing short stories for magazines. In these stories, many of which were later collected in two volumes, *Flappers and Philosophers* (1920) and *Tales of the Jazz Age* (1922), Fitzgerald continued to explore the world of the American aristocracy. As he would throughout the rest of his literary career, Fitzgerald borrowed experiences, events and people from his own life and incorporated them into his fiction.

His earlier short fiction during this period was light and amusing. His later stories, such as "Benediction" or "The Ice Palace," were more serious. As he began to master plot, Fitzgerald concentrated more heavily on character development. At the same time, one of his most notable talents was his ability to depict setting in realistic detail and make it come alive on the page. He wanted all his life to be considered a serious artist and had reservations about publishing stories in the popular magazines. But he and Zelda had expensive tastes, and even though *This Side of Paradise* was doing well, he needed to keep more money coming in, because they were going through it so fast.

After a trip to Europe, the Fitzgeralds settled briefly in St. Paul. There Fitzgerald worked on *Tales of the Jazz Age*, which was published just after *The Beautiful and Damned*. It was at this productive time that Zelda gave birth to their only child, a baby girl, Scottie.

St. Paul quickly became dull for Scott and Zelda, and so they moved to Great Neck, Long Island, in October of 1922. Great Neck Estates, where they rented an immense mansion, was home to numerous celebrities, and Scott and Zelda loved to entertain them. Their parties were wild, riotous affairs that sometimes lasted for days.

Again, Fitzgerald harvested rich material from his own life and used it in his fiction. "I believe that on the first night I went to Gatsby's house I was one of the few guests who had actually been invited," says Nick Carraway, the narrator of *The Great Gatsby* (1925), a novel that many consider to be Fitzgerald's most important work.

People were not invited—they went there. They got into automobiles which bore them out to Long Island, and somehow they ended up at Gatsby's door. Once there they were introduced by somebody who knew Gatsby, and after that they conducted themselves according to the rules of behavior associated with an amusement park . . . By midnight the hilarity had increased. A celebrated tenor had sung in Italian, and a notorious contralto had sung in jazz, and between the numbers people were doing "stunts" all over the garden, while happy vacuous bursts of laughter rose toward the summer sky.

While *This Side of Paradise* had been fresh and new and warmly received, its style was a bit sketchy, as if it were not quite finished or fully developed. With *The Great Gatsby*, however, Fitzgerald had reached a level of rich maturity in his writing. Told in a simple, elegant style, it is recognized as one of the greatest novels of American literature.

It is the story of Jay Gatsby, a mysterious millionaire who lives in a mansion on Long Island and throws lavish parties with the hope of attracting the attention of Daisy Buchanan, wife of Tom Buchanan, who lives across the harbor. Gatsby's neighbor happens to be Daisy's cousin, Nick Carraway, and Gatsby reveals to him that he and Daisy had a brief affair before she was married. Gatsby's background is shrouded in mystery, but it turns out that he actually comes from a poor family and earned his fortune through shady deals. His goal is to become the type of man Daisy respects, but he fails at winning her from her husband, Tom, who is suspicious of Gatsby. Daisy, while driving Gatsby's car, accidentally hits and kills Tom's mistress, Myrtle, and Myrtle's husband traces the car to Long Island and shoots Gatsby.

As a social novel, *Gatsby* is an examination of the bitter contrast between the old established wealth of the East and the new, burgeoning money of the West. Gatsby and Nick Carraway are both Westerners and live on West Egg, whereas Easterner Tom Buchanan of East Egg comes from old-family money. Buchanan's antagonism toward Gatsby reflects the resentment of his class toward a new and rising class of people in America who worked for their fortunes. Yet far from being an upright exemplar of his class's virtues, Buchanan is a cruel, bigoted, violent man who uses people for his own ends. Gatsby, on the other hand, while not entirely honest, suffers the tragic flaw of thinking that money can buy him anything he wishes—even his past happiness with Daisy.

More significantly, *The Great Gatsby* is an insightful look at a class and a generation of people who, with their wealth and energy, had tremendous potential but failed to achieve anything. Nick Carraway ponders at the end of the book: "[A]s I sat there brooding on the old, unknown world, I thought of Gatsby's wonder when he first picked out the green light at the end of Daisy's dock. He had come a long way to this blue lawn, and his dream must have seemed so close that he could hardly fail to grasp it. He did not know that it was already behind him . . ."

Elements of *The Great Gatsby*—a young man pretending to be something he is not, striving for recognition, in love with a girl beyond his reach, trying to realize the American dream of happiness through success and wealth, but ultimately experiencing tragedy—reflects events of Fitzgerald's personal history. These elements also provide the central theme for the novel, which is the pursuit of the romantic vision. "[T]he green light at the end of Daisy's dock" and indeed Daisy herself and her world, represented for Fitzgerald the essential disillusioning truth behind that vision, which reappears in Fitzgerald's fiction in such novels as *The Last Tycoon* (1941) or the short story "Babylon Revisited."

In 1924 the Fitzgeralds moved to Paris for an extended stay. Fitzgerald was now at the high point in his career. *The Great Gatsby* came out in the spring and received high praise from the critics and other well-established writers such as Edith Wharton, T. S. Eliot and Willa Cather. Fitzgerald had gone from earning $879 in 1919 to $28,760 in 1923, although he and Zelda hadn't managed to save a cent of it. They maintained their wild life-style, and Fitzgerald called the summer of 1925 the summer of "1000 parties and no work." It was a remarkable time to be in Paris. Owing to a strong dollar, many Americans had flocked there to enjoy the high living their money could buy. There were also numerous artists and writers, both native and expatriate, haunting the bistros and cafes along the famous Left Bank of the river Seine.

One of those writers, a journalist for the Toronto *Star*, was the young Ernest Hemingway, whom Fitzgerald met in a bar in the spring of 1925. They were an odd pair: Fitzgerald the sensitive, dandyish, Ivy League drop-out, yearning for acceptance, and Hemingway, the rugged, manly, self-confident newspaper man with a taste for bullfights and boxing. In truth, they had more admiration for each other's work than their personalities. In the beginning, Hemingway, who had yet to publish his first novel, looked up to Fitzgerald, the accomplished writer. (Indeed, it was Fitzgerald who brought Hemingway's writing to the attention of Maxwell Perkins at Scribner's.)

But in time the tables turned, and it was Fitzgerald who leaned on Hemingway's strength during periods of uncertainty. The two would maintain this love/hate relationship the rest of their lives.

Another love/hate relationship that had been brewing was Fitzgerald's marriage to Zelda. The two of them had caroused and cavorted their way through Paris and along the fashionable French Riviera, and it was all beginning to take its toll.

"They complemented each other like gin and vermouth in a martini," wrote Fitzgerald's friend and biographer Andrew

Turnbull, "each making the other more powerful in their war with dullness and convention."

Tired of simply being the subject of her husband's writing, Zelda wanted something to do of her own. She tried ballet, writing and even a love affair. The Fitzgeralds returned to America in 1926, and by 1930, with Zelda on the verge of a nervous breakdown, Fitzgerald admitted her to an asylum.

He chose the best one he could find, in Switzerland, and he stayed there writing magazine stories, which brought him up to $4,000 a piece. He desperately needed the money to pay for Zelda's hospital bills. She was released in 1931 but had a relapse the following year, and Fitzgerald committed her to a hospital in Baltimore, Maryland.

He rented a house nearby and continued to churn out what he considered "absolute junk" for the magazines. Some of this "junk" were articles he wrote simply for the money, but there were stories too, such as "Family in the Wind," "Crazy Sunday" and perhaps the finest, "Babylon Revisited."

These stories represent a turning point in Fitzgerald's career. Written at a time when Zelda's illness was putting him under extreme emotional and financial pressure, and when he was just turning the corner of what would eventually be his decline, these stories, unlike many of the others he had written to date, are not so much concerned with the sentimental past as they are with the unhappy present. Some of the stories would later be collected in *Taps at Reveille* (1935).

But while he was writing short fiction, he had in mind another novel. *Tender Is the Night*, not surprisingly, was about a young female mental patient, Nicole, who falls in love with her psychiatrist, Dick Diver—a character Fitzgerald modeled on himself.

Tender Is the Night was published in the spring of 1934 to mixed reviews. Many of Fitzgerald's intellectual friends thought it a significant achievement, but the reading public was less enthusiastic. This was not only a disappointment to Fitzgerald but also a matter of true concern since he had gone desperately into debt with Scribner's and his literary agent to the tune of some $40,000. The magazines were paying less and less for his stories, and he was forced to sell to lesser known publications for a fraction of what he had been accustomed to earning. He suffered from severe bouts of insecurity and drank all day instead of working. What stories he did manage to produce and send off to his agent were sometimes so disjointed, scratched-out and stained that they were unreadable.

F. Scott Fitzgerald

Desperate, lonely and nearing mental and physical exhaustion, Fitzgerald fled to a cheap hotel in a small, obscure town where he wrote an essay called "The Crack Up." Returning to Baltimore, he wrote two more essays on the same subject. "The Crack Up" series was a confession of his insecurities as a writer and his dependence on others for his sense of well-being. When the articles appeared in *Esquire* magazine, Hemingway was disgusted with what he considered Fitzgerald's "whining in public."

At possibly his lowest ebb, Fitzgerald got one more chance in June of 1937 to get out of debt and perhaps win back his self-re-

By 1937—the year this photo was taken—Fitzgerald's career had bottomed out. His wife had been committed to an asylum, his books weren't selling, and heavy debts forced him to go to Hollywood to write screenplays. Like his own character Gatsby, however, he was usually able to muster a brave smile in the face of adversity.
(National Archives)

spect. His agent managed to get him a contract with Metro-Gold-wyn-Mayer writing screenplays at $1,000 a week, and Fitzgerald moved to Hollywood.

He soon discovered that writing for the movies was vastly different than writing novels and short stories. Directors slashed much of his complex dialogue, and he became frustrated, angry and difficult to work with. He knew that this job was all he had going for him, though, and so he stuck with it as best he could.

Meanwhile, his relationship with Zelda was, for all practical purposes, over. He wrote her doctor, saying that he couldn't take care of her ever again and that each time he saw her it made the both of them unhappy. In his letter (quoted in Andrew Turnbull's *Scott Fitzgerald*), he said that he "had an ache for the beautiful child that I had loved and with whom I was happy as I shall never be again." He continued to send money for her expenses, as well as those of his daughter Scottie, who was then in school.

At the end of 1938, Fitzgerald's contract with MGM was not renewed. He found work at another studio, but this soon fizzled out, and he was through with the movies.

"Now was the time," writes Turnbull, "of hospitals, nurses, night sweats and despair." He fell into a slow decline of drinking himself to death, unable to write, half-crazed and suicidal. He was reduced to begging for advance money (a mere $500 once) from his agent for stories he had in mind but hadn't yet written. His requests were refused. Although he had nine books in print, his total royalties from them in 1939 was a pathetic $33.

But Fitzgerald still had the drive to write and felt that he had one last novel left in him. Based on the short, tragic career of Hollywood producer Irving Thalberg, *The Last Tycoon*, like *Gatsby*, would look at the rise and fall of an American dream. Unfinished, it was Fitzgerald's last work.

In November of 1940, he had a heart attack, but survived. His doctor told him that he had to rest for six weeks. He seemed to be recovering, but on December 20 he suffered another attack. The next afternoon, while eating a chocolate bar and making some notes on Princeton's football team for the upcoming year (he was still an avid fan), he suddenly stood up, grasped the mantelpiece in his Hollywood apartment and fell to the floor, gasping for breath. In a moment, he was dead. He was 44 years old.

Between the lines of F. Scott Fitzgerald's fiction we can clearly read his meteoric rise and tragic fall, but, woven into the body of his work, we can also find a powerful era in America's history. He emerged on the scene during a time of incredible economic, industrial and technical growth. America, shaking off the dust of the 19th century with great hope for the future, had gone into the "Roaring Twenties" with bright expectations of better, wealthier days to come. The devastating economic crash of October 1929 and the Great Depression that followed crushed many of these hopes.

During this bleak period Fitzgerald's popularity waned, in part because he was so associated with the high living of the earlier half of the decade. Yet what the public failed to realize was that, in chronicling his own decline, Fitzgerald was writing about the decline of that hopeful generation of Americans to which he was inextricably connected.

Perhaps his greatest strength was as a social novelist, a scrutinizer of and commentator on American society. He was one of the first American writers to closely examine the concept of class, and he did it perceptively again and again in his fiction. Indeed, he once claimed that writers have only one story to tell, and he did so by looking at it, as one would a gem, from different angles and in different light, reporting on its multiple facets, glints and gleams in great detail.

He did not take this look from a safe distance, but instead hurled himself, physically, financially and emotionally, into the world he was writing about so that it became hard to determine where F. Scott Fitzgerald ended and Jay Gatsby or Dick Diver began. It was the authenticity of this testimony that captured the interest and the excitement of his generation and assured him of his place in the canon of American literature. Although he is sometimes criticized for being limited in scope, he was nonetheless an indisputably good storyteller. Today, he is considered one of the greatest of American writers, and *The Great Gatsby* remains required reading in many high schools.

Fitzgerald's life and work are often compared with those of his friend and contemporary Ernest Hemingway. Both were members of what the great American literary guru, Gertrude Stein, is credited with calling "the Lost Generation"—a group of disillusioned young men and women who came of age during World War I and wandered in search of truth.

One of Fitzgerald's recent biographers, André Le Vot, draws a parallel between Fitzgerald and Hemingway and two literary giants of the 19th century, Henry James and Mark Twain. Hemingway, like Twain, turned his back on society to travel and then criticize what he had left behind from a safe distance. Like James, Fitzgerald immersed himself in that society and looked at it from the inside out. It was a vision that bore him to the highest peak of his generation's achievement and then dashed him, like a wave, against the rocks of its failure.

Chronology

September 24, 1896	born in St. Paul, Minnesota
1909	publishes first story, "The Mystery of Raymond Mortgage"
1913	enters Princeton
1917–18	leaves Princeton without a degree, joins the Army; meets Zelda Sayre; begins work on first novel, titled *The Romantic Egoist*
1920	publishes tremendously successful first novel, retitled *This Side of Paradise*; marries Zelda
1921–22	daughter Scottie born, family moves to Great Neck; *The Beautiful and Damned*; *Tales of the Jazz Age*
1924	moves to Paris
1925	meets Hemingway; *The Great Gatsby*
1930–34	Zelda suffers series of breakdowns; *Tender Is the Night* (1934)
1937	works at MGM as screenwriter
1939	begins writing *The Last Tycoon*
December 21, 1940	dies of a heart attack in Hollywood, California

Further Reading

Fitzgerald's Works

This Side of Paradise (New York: Charles Scribner's Sons, 1920). Fitzgerald's first novel and the one that launched his career.

The Great Gatsby (New York: Charles Scribner's Sons, 1925). Fitzgerald's classic story of life and love in the Roaring Twenties.

The Stories of F. Scott Fitzgerald: A Selection of 28 Stories, with introduction by Malcolm Cowley (Collier Books/Macmillan, 1986). The stories in this volume cover two decades of Fitzgerald's career. A lengthy introduction by Cowley puts Fitzgerald and his work in perspective.

Books About Fitzgerald

Matthew J. Bruccoli, *Scott and Ernest* (Carbondale and Edwardsville: Southern Illinois University Press, 1978). Evenhanded, critical study of one of the most famous literary friendships of all time.

Richard Lehan, *The Great Gatsby: The Limits of Wonder* (Boston: Twayne, 1990). This study of Fitzgerald's masterpiece weaves together cultural and biographical information; also includes a detailed chronology. Another in Twayne's Masterwork Studies series.

Arthur Mizener, *The Far Side of Paradise* (Boston: Houghton Mifflin, 1949). The first biography of F. Scott Fitzgerald. Considered a standard.

Andrew Turnbull, *Scott Fitzgerald* (New York: Charles Scribner's Sons, 1962). An intimate, though somewhat biased biography, written by a friend of Fitzgerald's.

William Faulkner
(1897–1962)

The silver-haired man of letters and southern gentleman, William Faulkner, photographed at the time of his professorship at the University of Virginia. Faulkner wasn't always quite so distinguished. His was a lifelong struggle for recognition, and in his youth he was considered a no-account radical.
(Library of Congress)

Of all the great American writers of the early 20th century, no one of them casts a longer shadow than William Faulkner. His fiction is populated by an enormous lineage of memorable characters who exist in a complex world. It was a world that Faulkner fashioned from the landmarks of his family history and the memories of his own life-experiences in the Deep South.

Faulkner's books shocked the reading public and alienated many of his neighbors. By peeling back the thin, yellowing veneer of southern gentility, he revealed the rotting social framework that existed underneath—a framework infested by racism, violence, incest and corruption.

Taking his lead from contemporary Irish novelist and short-story writer James Joyce, Faulkner advanced the technique of "stream of consciousness," in which the inner, unedited thoughts of a character are explored in detail. His long, meandering sentences became stylistic trademarks and reflected the oral tradition he drew upon to develop his unique and powerful style.

"I listen to the voices," Faulkner once said about the creative process that took place in his head when he wrote. These voices echoed all the way back to the time of his great ancestor, Colonel William C. Falkner, a Civil War hero whose statue loomed large over the graveyard in Ripley, Mississippi.

William Cuthbert Falkner was born on September 25, 1897, in New Albany, Mississippi. (Faulkner added the "u" to his name when he joined the Royal Air Force, in an effort to assume a new identity.) His father, Murray Falkner, was an alcoholic, prone to violent rampages and young Bill often sought refuge in the arms of his mother, Maud. It was Maud who first introduced Bill to literature. Another nurturing member of the Falkner household was Mammy Callie, a beloved old black servant.

Faulkner continued to read in the library at his grandfather's house where he loved to hear stories of the heroic "Old Colonel" Falkner. In his idle hours—and he had plenty, as he was a poor student who never did much school work—young Bill sat outside the courthouse listening to the old men swap tales of their victories on the battlefield or recount family legends.

He hung on every word and was soon telling stories himself, mingling fact with fiction. He would later recall the family histories of Oxford and weave them into his complicated cycle of Yoknapatawpha stories, which chronicled the entire history of a fictional Mississippi county.

Besides Maud Falkner, one person who had hope for Bill was Phil Stone, son of a well-to-do family friend of the Falkner's. A scholar of English and Greek literature and a graduate of Yale, Stone met Bill in 1914 and saw great potential in the would-be writer. All the boy needed was a little culture. Stone took over the youth's education by introducing him to the English Romantic poets and lecturing him on literature and the fine arts. These lessons often took place while driving through the countryside in Stone's Studebaker or in the drawing room of the Stone family mansion.

In addition to these tutoring sessions, Faulkner spent his time going on hunting trips into the woods, where he listened closely to the tales told around the campfires at night. One story he especially enjoyed hearing concerned a bear named Old Reel Foot, who was said to have outwitted hunters for years and once almost wiped out a whole pack of dogs with his deadly claws. Old Reel Foot would appear as Old Ben in one of Faulkner's most famous stories, "The Bear" (1941).

Another element of the hunting trips that Bill enjoyed was the passing around of the whiskey jug, and Maud watched in horror as her son began to develop a taste for alcohol just like his father. The boy needed straightening out, and his grandfather took charge by getting Bill a job as a bookkeeper. Bill hated the job, continued to drink even more and was finally devastated by the news that his childhood sweetheart, Estelle Oldham, was engaged to marry a boy she had met at the University of Mississippi (or "Ole Miss" as it was called).

Bill felt there was nothing left for him in Mississippi. In April of 1918, he decided he would go off to battle, like his great-grandfather before him, to die a glorious death. His field of battle would be in the skies over Europe, as America had just entered World War I. He had visions of being a flying ace but was too scrawny to join the American forces. Phil Stone suggested he try the British Royal Air Force, which was signing up recruits in Canada.

Bill lied about his background at the recruiting station, saying he had been born in England and that his name was William "Faulkner." He trained for five months to be a flyer but never got off the ground because the war ended soon after he finished his training. Back in Oxford, this didn't stop him from telling exciting and entirely fabricated tales of how he had crashed and injured his leg while performing daring aerial stunts. He continued to embellish his war story throughout his life, telling some people that he had actually fought in Europe and had a metal plate in his head as a result of being wounded in a crash.

He resumed his tutelage under Stone, and began reading such contemporary poets as Robert Frost and Edwin Arlington Robinson. By spring of 1919, he was inspired enough to send some of his own poems to *The New Republic*, which accepted one, "L'Aprés-midi d'un Faune," a romantic piece about a nymph and a faun. Faulkner's first published work appeared in the August 6, 1919, issue.

This minor success wasn't nearly enough to convince Murray Falkner that his eldest son was destined to be a poet. Murray made Faulkner enroll at Ole Miss, where the boy studied English as a non-degree student. Though Faulkner seldom made it to class, he frequently contributed stories and poems to the school newspaper. He also formed a drama group with one of his few friends at college, Ben Wasson, a young man from Greenville, Mississippi, with whom he shared a fondness for poetry, liquor and poker.

Having accomplished little in the way of a formal education, Faulkner withdrew from Ole Miss in November of 1920. He returned home and became the bohemian poet, walking through the streets of Oxford barefoot, with rags for clothing and his hair sticking out wildly from his head. His uncle John Falkner (as quoted in Stephen B. Oates's *William Faulkner, The Man and the Artist*) summed up his nephew's character by saying "[t]hat damn Billy is not worth a Mississippi goddamn."

Faulkner's uncle seemed to have had a point. Aside from writing poetry, Faulkner's favorite pastime was driving up to Memphis, Tennessee, with Stone to drink bootleg whiskey and cruise the cat houses. After a brief, aborted attempt to establish himself in New York City as a writer, he returned to Oxford, where he got a job in the local post office.

Faulkner treated this job with the same degree of enthusiasm he had for work in general. Instead of waiting on customers he often closed the customer window and sat there reading poetry; when people clamored for service he simply ignored them. He was desperate to be published again, and Stone came to his rescue once more, offering to pay to have a collection of Faulkner's poems published. Stone even wrote a preface for *The Marble Faun* (1924), in which he stated that the new, young Southern poet showed great "promise." Faulkner was proud of this little volume of poetry and was happier still when he finally got fired from his job at the post office.

"Thank God I won't ever again have to be at the beck and call of every son of a bitch who's got two cents to buy a stamp," he said of his dismissal.

In November of 1924 Faulkner went to New Orleans, where he met the popular author Sherwood Anderson. The two took to each other right away, and Anderson eventually did much to advance Faulkner's career, just as he did for Hemingway's. It was Anderson who encouraged Faulkner to write about "that little patch up there in Mississippi where you started from."

But Faulkner turned to his experiences as a cadet in the RAF for the material of his first novel. *Soldier's Pay* (1926) was accepted by Anderson's publisher, Boni & Liveright, upon Anderson's recommendation. (By this time, Anderson and Faulkner had grown distant, and the author of *Winesburg, Ohio* said he was willing to do Faulkner the favor as long as he didn't have to read the "damn manuscript." In 1926, Faulkner parodied Anderson in his introduction to *Sherwood Anderson and Other Famous Creoles*, a collection of caricatures that severed the friendship for good.)

Faulkner was in Paris when he received the delightful news that his novel was to be published. He had gone to Europe to soothe a broken heart over a failed relationship and to rub elbows with the "Lost Generation" of expatriate writers. He spent more of his time loitering on a bench in the Luxembourg Gardens smoking a pipe and fingering his new beard, which he thought made him look distinguished.

Back in New Orleans he got to work on his next book, *Mosquitoes* (1927), also published by Boni & Liveright. Neither *Mosquitoes* nor *Soldier's Pay* are considered among Faulkner's best novels. Still, their frank language and narrative structures provide us with hints of what Faulkner was capable of. At home in Oxford, people simply considered his books "dirty."

Faulkner took a harder look at "that little patch" in Mississippi in his next novel, which examined the degeneration of an old Southern family named Sartoris, based on Faulkner's own family history. Colonel John Sartoris's descendant Bayard, home from World War I, is wracked with guilt over the death of his brother John and sets out on a path of self-destruction that eventually causes his grandfather, Bayard, to die of a heart attack. He marries Narcissa Benbow but is himself killed in a plane crash.

Sartoris (1929) is significant in that it is the first of Faulkner's novels to take place in the imaginary Yoknapatawpha County where the writer set most of his fiction. Faulkner's portrayal of this place—with its county seat of Jefferson (based on Oxford), its Negro quarter, its rivers, swamps, plantations, its inhabitants and their complex relationships—is so arrestingly realistic (Faulkner even provided population figures) that numerous books have been written on this aspect of his work alone.

It is an indication of the remarkable level of retention and imagination Faulkner possessed that he could create in his fiction an entire section of the country, complete with its own history and literally hundreds of characters.

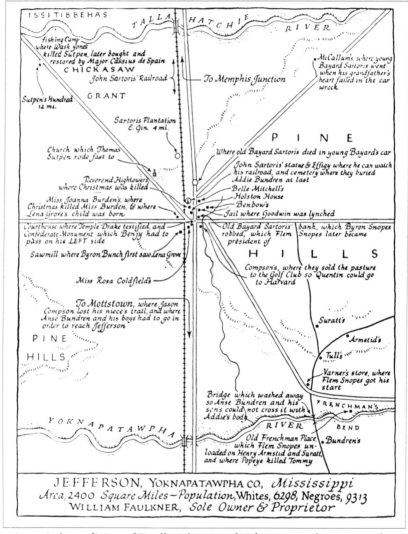

An artist's rendition of Faulkner's map of Yoknapatawpha County that appeared in the original edition of Absalom, Absalom! *Faulkner's fictitious landscape was so detailed it included population figures.* (Courtesy Random House)

Faulkner had a hard time interesting a publisher in *Sartoris*. Harcourt, Brace finally decided to take a chance, but still wasn't interested in *The Sound and the Fury* (1929), Faulkner's new and unusual book about the decline of the aristocratic Compson family. Quentin, Jason and Benjy are brothers; gentle, loving Caddy is their sister. The novel is divided into four sections, with the first three told through the interior monologues of the Compson brothers. The last is from the point of view of Dilsey Gibson, the old black cook, based on Faulkner's memories of Mammy Callie.

Benjy is an idiot, cared for and protected by Caddy, as in the book's opening pages where the Compsons, as children, are scurrying underneath a fence: *"Caddy uncaught me and we crawled through. Uncle Maury said to not let anybody see us, so we better stoop over, Caddy said. Stoop over, Benjy. Like this, see."*

Quentin is a Harvard student, plagued by guilt over his incestuous fantasies about his sister and tortured by his hypochondriac mother and drunken father. He finally drowns himself. Mean-spirited Jason, now the head of the family, mistreats Benjy and hates Caddy and her illegitimate daughter, whom she's named Quentin.

"Once a bitch always a bitch, what I say" is Jason's view of the young Quentin, as well as of the kind-hearted but formidable Dilsey Gibson whom Jason lacks the courage to banish from the house. She is the Compson family's last link with the glory and honor of its past. Her story is told on Easter, which, Oates observes, "suggested the possibility of redemption, the continuation of the human story . . ." It is Dilsey, with her courage and strength, who prevails in the face of the Compson family's self-destruction.

"'I've seen de first en de last,'" she says. "'I seed de beginnin, en now I sees de endin.'"

Public reception of *The Sound and the Fury* was mixed. The reviews were generally favorable, and comparisons to Joyce were inevitable. However, as Frederick R. Karl observed in his biography *William Faulkner: American Writer*, "some critics . . . felt the Joyce connection only made Faulkner as incoherent as the Irish writer" and thus "the attachment was disadvantageous."

Faulkner had definitely given the reading public something new and unfamiliar to deal with. Ben Wasson, then Faulkner's literary agent, tried to make sense of the manuscript by separating italicized parts from the main body of the text with section breaks. Faulkner angrily told him to take out the breaks and leave the manuscript as it was. He knew that it was crucial for readers to hear the voices in their heads, just as he had when he wrote down their words. As Frederick R. Karl points out, *The Sound and the Fury* is ostensibly a novel about the South, but it is also "about language, voices, speech, expression, temporal relationships." Faulkner himself observed, "[w]e need to talk, to tell, since oratory is our heritage."

People in Oxford, Mississippi, were certainly talking about Bill Faulkner. Not only was he the author of those "dirty" books, but he was also frequently seen in the company of Estelle Franklin, whose marriage had not worked out. As soon as she had freed herself of her husband, she was desperate for Faulkner to marry her. She now had two children and needed the support of family life.

By this time, however, Faulkner wasn't so sure he wanted to marry Estelle. Earlier women and relationships had left him with a bitter taste in his mouth, but Estelle pleaded and he finally gave in. It was perhaps one of the biggest mistakes in his life, since the two of them were hardly compatible. She was a gaudy extrovert, while he was reclusive and moody.

There was also the issue of money. Estelle's first husband had been a prosperous businessman, and she was used to luxury. Faulkner at this point was working the night shift at a power plant and writing during the day. But when he began to sell some of his stories to the popular magazines, he felt secure enough to purchase an old mansion surrounded by a few wooded acres. He called his new home Rowan Oak. The place needed a few things—such as plumbing and electricity—but it appealed to Faulkner's sense of history and romance. Estelle spent much of her first week there sitting on the sagging porch, crying.

But Faulkner wasn't paying attention to Estelle's tears. He was listening to the "voices" again, and this time they were telling him about the death of a hateful, bitter woman, Addie Bundren, and of the ordeal her family goes through getting her body to Jefferson for burial in the family plot.

As I Lay Dying (1930) is one of Faulkner's most disturbing, yet most comic novels. Addie's husband, Anse, is a toothless and twisted old man who looks on the bright side of his wife's death: Since they'll be going to town, he'll be able to pick up a set of dentures he's been wanting.

"'God's will be done,'" he says, standing over his wife's body. "'Now I can get them teeth.'"

The other characters in the novel—Addie's children Cash, Darl, Jewel, Vardaman and Dewey, as well as several neighbors—explain their relationships to her through stream-of-consciousness monologues. Each chapter bears the name of the character whose mind and thoughts are being revealed.

It took Faulkner just six weeks to write this brilliantly innovative novel. He sent it off with high hopes to Hal Smith of Cape and Smith, the firm that had published *The Sound and the Fury*. Smith agreed to publish the book, but expressed his interest in another that Faulkner had once showed him. It was called *Sanctuary* (1931) and it was, as Faulkner himself said, "a shocker."

Faulkner had written the book two years earlier but had put it aside, feeling it either needed more work or should just be destroyed. Inspired by Smith's interest, he decided to rewrite his story of a young coed, Temple Drake, who is raped with a corncob by the vicious Popeye. Popeye murders a half-wit who is trying to protect Temple, then drags her off to a brothel where he watches her making love to another man. Meanwhile, intellectual Horace Benbow (whose sister Narcissa had appeared in *Sartoris*) tries to defend Lee Goodwin, accused of killing the half-wit and raping Temple. Benbow believes he has a case until Temple perjures herself and testifies that it was Goodwin and not Popeye who committed the crimes. Goodwin is then lynched.

Faulkner was right about *Sanctuary* being a "shocker." The critics questioned its taste, but the public ate it up. As Oates notes, the book sold more copies in its first three weeks than *The Sound and the Fury* and *As I Lay Dying* had since their publication.

A sad event intruded on Faulkner's success with *Sanctuary*: His first child with Estelle, a little girl named Alabama, died 10 days after she was born. Faulkner was shattered by the loss, and for once in his life he refused to turn to the bottle to help him overcome his grief.

Faulkner's next novel, *Light in August* (1932), was the most complex he had attempted to date. Joe Christmas is the central character in this powerful book, which deals with one of the South's most sensitive issues—race. Christmas appears white but has black blood in his veins, and this is enough to condemn him in Yoknapatawpha County. He has an affair with Joanna Burden, but then resents her kindness to him. He kills her and burns down her house, then flees. He is captured, castrated and then killed by the angry townspeople, who feel his crime and his black blood justify his death. Other characters are Lena Grove, a pregnant woman in search of the man who seduced her, and Gail Hightower, a minister so tied to the past that he loses everything he has in the present.

The characters in *Light in August* are on journeys of self-discovery and fulfillment. "A body does get around," concludes Lena Grove. Joe Christmas's journey is wrought with tension and conflict, in which the "white blood" struggles against the "black blood" in him: "[H]is blood would not be quiet . . . It would not be either one or the other and let his body save itself." The book reflected Faulkner's critical views of southern society, which harshly judged men by the color of their skin. In the end, Joe Christmas the victim becomes Joe Christmas the triumphant, but death is the price he must pay for his victory.

Although his productivity was up, Faulkner's bank account was running low. Aside from *Sanctuary*, his books weren't selling well. Desperate for cash, Faulkner made a fateful decision in the spring of 1932 to accept an offer to write screenplays for Metro-Goldwyn-Mayer studios in Hollywood.

He hated the work and had no idea at the time that he would be financially dependent on the movie business, off and on, for the next 20 years of his life. In all, Faulkner worked on some 50 screenplays and treatments, including the adaptations of several of his own novels. Two people in Hollywood who helped him keep his sanity were the famous director Howard Hawks, who became a close friend and supporter, and Hawks's personal secretary, Meta Carpenter, with whom Faulkner eventually had a long, passionate affair.

By the following year, the author of *Sanctuary* was so fed up with the movie business that all he could think about was going back to Mississippi. In a story that has since become Hollywood legend, Faulkner finally asked one of the studio heads if he could work at home, meaning Oxford. The studio executive thought that by "home" Faulkner meant his Hollywood apartment, and gave his consent. Months later, when the MGM brass learned that Faulkner was drawing a salary without even being in the state, let alone on the studio lot, they angrily let him go. Although Faulkner often liked to recount this story, the truth was that Howard Hawks and at least one other executive had worked out the long-distance work arrangement with Faulkner, but he was fired nevertheless.

This was nothing but a relief to Faulkner who was happy to be back in Oxford in June of 1933 for the birth of another daughter, Jill. He had earned enough money to survive for a while, thanks to screenwriting as well as the sale of the movie rights to *Sanctuary*. He began work then on *Requiem for a Nun* (finally published in 1951), a continuation of the Temple Drake story, but put it aside to write one of his most famous novels, *Absalom, Absalom!* (1936). *Absalom, Absalom!* introduces yet another Yoknapatawpha family, the Sutpens, and its patriarch, Colonel Thomas Sutpen, who is descended from poor whites. The book follows Sutpen's attempts to raise his family name to a position of honor. These plans are thwarted when Sutpen's son runs off after killing his part-black half brother, Charles Bon, Sutpen's illegitimate son. In the end, the Colonel's only living descendant is an idiot black man, Jim Bond, left howling in the ashes of the burned Sutpen mansion. The story is told by several narrators, including Quentin Compson, from *The Sound and the Fury*.

Financial pressures forced Faulkner back to Hollywood in February of 1936, this time to work for Twentieth Century–Fox, where he resentfully wrote more screenplays and drank heavily to ease his frustration. He followed up *Absalom, Absalom!* with *The Unvanquished* (1938), a collection of stories, first serialized in magazines, concerning the Civil War–era history of the *Sartoris* family. Back at Rowan Oak, he began writting *The Wild Palms* (1939), a curious novel that incorporates a second novel, *The Old Man*, between chapters. Exploring the history of yet another Yoknapatawpha family, Faulkner wrote *The Hamlet* (1940), the first of three planned novels dealing with the Snopes, the county's most reviled and vicious family of poor whites. *The Town* (1957) and *The Mansion* (1959) are the other books in the Snopes trilogy.

Faulkner's reputation was now growing. In 1939 he was elected to the National Institute of Arts and Letters. *Time* magazine, in a cover story, ranked him with Twain and Melville and called him "the most talented but least predictable Southern writer." Although he remained obscure and unreadable to many critics, it was clear that he had become "a modern master," as Karl puts it.

A hunting trip in November of 1940 rekindled Faulkner's interest in the story of Old Reel Foot, the almost mythical bear who wipes out packs of dogs with a swipe of his claws and eludes hunters for generations. Faulkner saw the bear as a powerful symbol of nature and of an ancient time when man had more regard for nature's laws.

In "The Bear," Faulkner wrote about how all this was changing, about the "doomed wilderness whose edges were being constantly and punily gnawed at by men with plows and axes who feared it because it was wilderness . . ."

73

"The Bear" is a classic rite-of-passage story in which young Ike McCaslin is taught respect for the woods as well as for Old Ben, the bear, by the Indian guide, Sam Fathers. Fathers, a symbol of man's relationship with nature, is so connected with the wilderness that when Old Ben is finally killed, he himself dies.

But Ike has learned his lessons well. In a brilliantly written piece of stream-of-consciousness, Faulkner explores Ike's past and the history of his family, which Ike now knows he must "relinquish." It is a history tainted by fatal lust and shame, recorded in the pages of dusty ledger books. Recurring themes in this section emphasize the sanctity of land and life and the absurdity of man's claims over either. In the final section of the story, Ike returns to the woods an older man, but knows that it will never be the same again, that he "would return no more."

"The Bear" appeared in *Go Down, Moses and Other Stories* (1942), which also included "Pantaloon in Black," one of several stories in the collection about blacks.

In 1942, Faulkner was roped into a seven-year screenwriting contract with Warner Brothers, owing to the poor judgment of his Hollywood agent. Faulkner was outraged at the deal, which paid only $300 a week. His one consolation in returning to Hollywood was his relationship with Meta.

Back at Rowan Oak on a couple of leaves of absence, Faulkner happily worked on a fable about Christ appearing on the battlefields of the First World War, an idea suggested by a Hollywood producer. The producer wanted a synopsis and screenplay, but Faulkner saw a novel coming out of the idea. He butted heads with the studio when he learned that, as part of his contract, Warner Brothers had first rights to anything he wrote. This was so intolerable that Faulkner simply cleaned out his desk one September day in 1945 and walked off the lot. The studio threatened to sue if he tried to sell any of his writing to someone else, but eventually relinquished rights to his metaphorical story of Christ, *A Fable* (1954), with the understanding that Faulkner would come back to Hollywood when he finished the book. The studio lawyers added this clause to save face, but both they and Faulkner knew he would never return.

In contrast to Warner Brothers' treatment of Faulkner, the literary editor of *The New Republic*, Malcolm Cowley, was much kinder. Cowley was "beginning to see a pattern that lay behind" Faulkner's books and considered this pattern brilliant. He said so in no uncertain terms in a long essay published in *The New*

Republic and excerpted in *The New York Times Book Review*. Cowley's critical observations caused the literary critics to wake up and take another look at Faulkner and increasingly to recognize his genius.

Cowley edited and wrote an introduction for *The Portable Faulkner* (1946), in which he stated that "the living pattern" of Faulkner's works was his "real achievement" and that "each novel, each long or short story, seems to reveal more than it states explicitly and to have a subject bigger than itself. All the separate works are like blocks of marble from the same quarry . . ."

Cowley, as Oates has observed, almost single-handedly reversed "the critical indifference to Faulkner's art." His opinions of Faulkner were later supported by the Pulitzer Prize–winning novelist and poet Robert Penn Warren, who also wrote an influential essay on Faulkner for *The New Republic*. Cowley and Faulkner became close friends through their correspondence, years before ever meeting each other.

In 1948, Faulkner sold the movie rights to his latest novel, *Intruder in the Dust*, for $50,000—a welcome boost to his income that allowed him to once and for all forget his contract with Warner Brothers. Also that year he was elected to the American Academy of Arts and Letters. At 50, he was beginning to feel worn out. He finally had a bit of financial security, but remained dissatisfied with life in general. Now a sought-after celebrity, he posted a "NO TRESPASSING" sign at the end of his driveway, hoping that the world that had shunned him for so long would now simply leave him alone. Despite the sign, he would still come across perfect strangers sneaking onto the grounds of Rowan Oak, hoping to catch a glimpse of the famous writer or perhaps to steal some personal item—his eyeglasses, a magazine, a drinking glass—which he may have left beside a lawn chair.

One of these intruders was a young girl from Memphis named Joan Williams, who arrived at Faulkner's gate in the summer of 1949. She was a student at Bard College in New York State and wanted to be a writer. The moment Faulkner set eyes on her youthful face he was smitten. Although old enough to be her father, he began what turned out to be a rocky affair with her, acting as both her lover and mentor.

In November of 1950, Faulkner learned that he had won the 1949 Nobel Prize for literature. He went to Stockholm, accompanied by his daughter Jill, to receive his prize and mumbled an acceptance speech that hardly anyone at the ceremony could hear.

When the speech was reprinted in the papers the next morning, everyone was talking about the impact of Faulkner's words.

"There are no longer problems of the spirit" he had said. "There is only the question: When will I be blown up? Because of this, the young man or woman writing today has forgotten the problems of the human heart in conflict with itself which alone can make good writing because only that is worth writing about . . ."

He went on to state "that man will not merely endure: he will prevail. He is immortal, not because he alone among creatures has an inexhaustible voice, but because he has a soul, a spirit capable of compassion and sacrifice and endurance."

The Nobel Prize made Faulkner an even bigger celebrity than ever and he was hounded for interviews and appearances. But Faulkner wanted his private life left out of it. It was a life in a

Faulkner in Stockholm, 1950, receiving the Nobel Prize for literature from King Gustaf Adolf VI of Sweden. In his acceptance speech Faulkner said the only thing worth writing about was "the human heart in conflict with itself."
(National Archives)

downward spiral. He went to New York to work and to be near Joan Williams, but his relationship with her was dissolving. She cared for him, but their age difference began to be an issue. As usual, he eased his broken heart with bourbon. He was also suffering from memory losses, insomnia and injuries sustained from horseback-riding accidents and falling down drunk on several occasions. His editor and friend, Saxe Commins, nursed Faulkner through many a painful night when the trembling writer wouldn't go to sleep without a bottle next to his bed.

In January of 1953, Faulkner spent time in a New York sanitarium where he underwent agonizing electroshock therapy for his alcoholism. At the end of the year, he grudgingly accepted an offer from his old Hollywood friend, Howard Hawks, to accompany him to Paris and Egypt to work on the script of *Land of the Pharaohs*. They were in Switzerland en route to Cairo when Faulkner met another young admirer, Jean Stein, a 19-year-old American student studying in Paris. Faulkner predictably fell in love with her and saw her several times during the trip.

Hawks, exasperated with Faulkner's drinking, finally just let him go. Faulkner returned to Paris to be with Jean and was back at Rowan Oak in August of 1954 for Jill's wedding. In January 1955, Faulkner accepted the National Book Award for *A Fable*, which also won the Pulitzer Prize in fiction.

Since Faulkner was now being taught in college classrooms, it seemed appropriate that the esteemed Southern writer ought to be teaching in one. That was the opinion of the University of Virginia, which offered him a position in the English department as writer-in-residence for the spring term in 1957. Faulkner was generally shy about speaking in front of people, but all this job required of him was to stand at the head of a classroom and answer questions about his books. He took the offer and returned again the following year, finally accepting an appointment at the university in August of 1960. He published his last novel, *The Reivers*, in 1962.

By now, the snowy-haired, pipe-smoking man-of-letters was finally getting the recognition he deserved and the financial rewards of a long career. Royalties were rolling in, and the movie sales of several novels padded his bank account. His affair with Jean Stein, who was by then living in New York, ended unhappily, and Estelle finally offered Faulkner a divorce. Curiously enough, he declined. In spite of his affairs, he still loved Estelle, and he didn't want to be alone in his final years.

Faulkner now became a distinguished Southern gentleman. He enjoyed fox-hunting and had his eye on a Virginia plantation where he could ride over his land and recreate the bygone splendor of his ancestor, the Old Colonel. It was while he was riding at Rowan Oak in June 1962 that he was thrown from his horse and injured his back—one of several riding accidents in his later years that had done damage to his spine.

Confined to a bed, he took tranquilizers to relieve the pain, mixing them with his old standby, bourbon. By July 5, the pain was too much for him to bear and he was admitted to the hospital. He was also complaining of chest pains, but the doctor who looked at him found nothing wrong with his heart or blood pressure. About half past one the next morning, July 6, Faulkner suffered a heart attack and died. He was buried the next day in St. Peter's Cemetery in Oxford.

Faulkner's artistic achievement is all but indisputable. No other American writer has produced such a complex and consistently superior body of work in the course of a career. Aside from the sheer volume of Faulkner's output (some 37 novels, story collections and books of poetry) and the legacy of Yoknapatawpha, Faulkner's style was unlike that of any of his predecessors. His use of stream-of-consciousness and flashback, his intricate narrative structures and methods of characterization were far ahead of their time, and no American writer who has since experimented with these techniques has done so without being indebted in some measure to William Faulkner.

Faulkner, however—the shy, strange and tragic little man from Mississippi—would probably decline the gratitude. He once informed Malcolm Cowley that in the end he wished that only his works be remembered.

"It is my ambition," he wrote "to be, as a private individual, abolished and voided from history, leaving it markless, no refuse save the printed books; I wish I had enough sense to see ahead . . . and, like some of the Elizabethans, not signed them. It is my aim, and every effort bent, that the sum and history of my life, which in the same sentence is my obit and epitaph too, shall be them both: He made the books and he died."

Chronology

September 25, 1897	born William Falkner in New Albany, Mississippi
1902	moves to Oxford, Mississippi, with family
1918	joins British RAF in Canada, changes last name to "Faulkner"
1919	enrolls at University of Mississippi; first published work, the poem "L'Aprés-midi d'un Faune"
1924–25	first book, *The Marble Faun,* a collection of poems; moves to New Orleans and meets Sherwood Anderson
1926	*Sartoris* and *The Sound and the Fury,* the first novels of Yoknapatawpha
1932	goes to Hollywood as a screenwriter; *Light in August*
1936	*Absalom, Absalom!*
1946	publication of *The Portable Faulkner* inspires critical reappraisal of previous work
1950	awarded Nobel Prize for literature
1955	*The Fable* wins Pulitzer Prize
1957–58	writer-in-residence at University of Virginia
July 6, 1962	dies of heart attack

Further Reading

Faulkner's Works

William Faulkner: Novels 1930–1935 (New York: Pylon, 1985). A collection of the best of Faulkner's early novels: *As I Lay Dying, Sanctuary, Light in August.*

The Sound and the Fury (New York: Random House, 1984). A corrected edition of Faulkner's powerful novel on the decline of the Compson family. The text was edited by comparing Faulkner's original manuscript and his typed copy of the book.

Absalom, Absalom! (New York: Vintage Books, 1972). Another story of a Southern family in decay.

Go Down, Moses and Other Stories (New York: Random House, 1942). A collection of short fiction that includes one of Faulkner's best stories, "The Bear."

Books About Faulkner

Richard H. Brodhead, editor, *Faulkner, New Perspectives* (Englewood Cliffs, NJ: Prentice-Hall, 1983). A selection of scholarly essays; includes chronology and selected bibliography.

Cleanth Brooks, *William Faulkner: First Encounters* (New Haven: Yale University Press, 1983). An excellent study of Faulkner's life and works written for the general reader and the student coming to Faulkner for the first time.

John T. Mathews, *The Sound and the Fury: Faulkner and the Lost Cause* (Boston: Twayne, 1991). Thorough and detailed study of the novel; puts the book in literary and historical context; also examines characters and technique. Includes chronology and bibliography. Part of Twayne's Masterworks series.

Stephen B. Oates, *William Faulkner, The Man and the Artist* (New York: Harper & Row, 1987). The first, full-scale biography written for a general audience.

Robert Dale Parker, *Absalom! Absalom!: The Questioning of Fictions* (Boston: Twayne, 1991). Thorough and detailed study of the book, aimed at a "full range of readers, from thoughtful beginners to scholarly specialists." Another of Twayne's Masterworks series.

Ernest Hemingway
(1899–1961)

Ernest Hemingway in the prime of his life, writing For Whom the Bell Tolls. *His powerful new style of fiction would have a lasting impact on American literature.*
(National Archives)

*T*he young writer stepped bravely into the bullring waving a scarlet matador's cape in his hand. It was the summer of 1924 in Pamplona, Spain—"a sun-baked town high up in the hills of Navarre" and "the toughest bull fight town in the world," according to the writer. This morning, he was here to prove to his friends and to the thousands of spectators crowding the Plaza de Toros that he was just as tough.

The writer tensed as the animal was released from his pen and came stomping and snorting into the ring. As the angry bull circled closer, the writer barked, "Huh, toro, toro!" The beast charged and the writer suddenly found himself literally "catching the bull by the horns." Although the horns were padded, the bull was still a dangerous opponent and it was only through sheer force that the writer succeeded in wrestling the animal to the ground. He looked up at his astonished friends, a broad smile spreading across his sun-tanned, masculine face.

What lured young Ernest Hemingway to Spain that summer, and every summer thereafter for almost 10 years, was what lured him to all parts of the world for most of his life—his thirst for adventure.

Whether it was in the bullrings of Spain, the mountain regions of Montana, on the blue waters of the Caribbean or the savannas of Africa, Hemingway lived life to the fullest. His zest for living was reflected in the power and energy of his fiction, with its sweeping themes of human conflict, whether that conflict took place in the boundless wilderness or the confines of the bedroom. In addition, his neatly clipped prose became so distinctive that today literary contests are held to determine the best imitation of Hemingway's style.

Destined to become one of America's most celebrated writers, Ernest Miller Hemingway was born on July 21, 1899, in the suburban town of Oak Park, Illinois, about a half-hour northwest of Chicago. As soon as he was old enough to travel (a mere seven weeks), his father, Dr. Ed Hemingway, whisked him and the family off to a hunting camp near Walloon Lake in the woods of northern Michigan.

It was here that the Hemingways spent their summer vacations in a cottage called Windemere. Ed Hemingway taught his son woodlore and how to shoot, and young Ernest developed an early fondness for such masculinity-associated activities as hunting and camping.

He showed promise as a writer in high school, contributing to the school newspaper and literary magazine. His English teachers had praise for his stories, which they said were clear, well-plotted and free of the usual awkwardness of high-school writing.

He played football for Oak Park High and developed a lifelong fondness for boxing. His active summers at Walloon Lake made him a husky, well-proportioned youth, and he kept in shape during the school year by going into Chicago to spar in the gyms with professionals.

After high school, in June of 1917, he landed a cub reporter's position on the *Kansas City Star*, one of the leading papers in the country in those days. This experience with the discipline of journalism contributed significantly to Hemingway's development as a writer. Veteran staff reporters taught him how to write tight, declarative sentences and how to develop a narrative structure that would hold a reader's interest.

"Use short sentences. Use short first paragraphs. Use vigorous English, not forgetting to strive for smoothness," the stylebook in the newsroom advised him, and Hemingway studied it from cover to cover.

Although Hemingway enjoyed newspaper work, he felt the urge to get involved in World War I. Unfortunately, poor vision made him ineligible for combat duty. He got around his handicap by volunteering as a Red Cross ambulance driver, and by June 1918, he and several friends from the *Star* found themselves in the Italian town of Schio in the Dolomite Alps. The fighting there was so infrequent that they called their comfortable barracks with an Alpine view "the Schio Country Club."

Eager to get into action, Hemingway volunteered for duty on Italy's eastern front, passing out chocolates, cigarettes and postcards to the troops. There, on the night of July 8, near Fosalta di Piave, he was wounded in the legs by an exploding mortar shell as he was crawling through the trenches.

He spent four months recuperating from his wounds at the Red Cross hospital in Milan where he met and fell in love with "a beautiful night nurse" named Agnes von Kurowsky. After a brief return to the war, which ended in November, Hemingway went back home in January of 1919. He and Agnes wrote each other for a few months. By March, however, she informed him that she had fallen in love with an Italian officer. Hemingway was so devastated by the news that he was bed-ridden. If there was a bright side to any of this, it was that his war experiences and his affair with Agnes would provide the raw material for one of his greatest novels, *A Farewell to Arms* (1929).

Back in Oak Park, he enjoyed playing the role of the wounded war hero and worked on his first attempts at serious fiction. He tried selling some stories to the popular magazines of the day such as the *Saturday Evening Post*, but his work was rejected. He spent

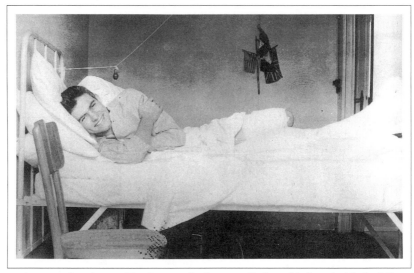

A young, handsome Hemingway flashes a smile from his hospital bed while recovering from wounds sustained on the World War I battlefields of Italy. It was in this hospital that he met and fell in love with a "beautiful night nurse." Their love affair would inspire Hemingway to write A Farewell to Arms.
(Hemingway Collection, John F. Kennedy Library)

the winter and spring in Toronto and took a job writing feature stories for *The Toronto Star Weekly*, while he continued to work on short fiction that just wouldn't sell.

Tiring of Canada, he eventually ended up in Chicago. He barely scraped by for several months, writing pieces for the *Toronto Star* and sparring in the gyms for money, before he got work on a monthly magazine called *The Cooperative Commonwealth*.

At a friend's party, Hemingway met the famous novelist and short story writer Sherwood Anderson, who became his mentor. The influence of Anderson's *Winesburg, Ohio*, with its focus on the individual in human relationships, can be seen in some of Hemingway's early short stories such as "The Three-Day Blow" or "The Doctor and the Doctor's Wife."

Another person Hemingway met in Chicago was a young girl visiting from St. Louis named Hadley Richardson. The two struck up a romance, which they continued by mail after Hadley returned to Missouri. They married in September of 1921 and, after living in Chicago for a short period, decided to go to Paris. Their decision had been greatly influenced by Sherwood Anderson, who armed Hemingway with letters of introduction to James Joyce's publisher, Sylvia Beach, poet Ezra Pound and Gertrude Stein, Paris's famed literary guru of the so-called "Lost Generation" of expatriates.

The newlyweds took an apartment in the city's fabled Latin Quarter, home to writers, artists and poets. They lived on a small trust fund of Hadley's, which Hemingway supplemented by writing feature stories for the *Toronto Daily Star* and *Star Weekly*.

The move to Paris was a key turning point in Hemingway's career. Although he continued to file news stories, he was gradually shifting his focus away from journalism to the craft of storytelling. Here, in the company of other great writers, Hemingway began to find a voice in his fiction. He abandoned his attempts to write the popular, more ornate prose being published in the slick magazines of the day. During the winter of 1922, he set out to write instead what he called "one true sentence"—a simple, declarative and unadorned statement of truth.

While he succeeded in publishing a few poems and stories in literary magazines, he still had to make a living, and so he covered various news events in Europe for the *Toronto Star*. He was in Lausanne covering a peace conference when he sent for Hadley to join him. On the train from Paris she lost a valise containing all of his fiction and poetry, with the exception of two stories—"Up in Michigan" and "My Old Man."

Having no choice but to start over again, Hemingway went to the Mediterranean town of Rapallo in Italy, where he got back to work. Here he met an editor, Edward O'Brien, who read and liked "My Old Man" so much that he decided to include it in *The Best Short Stories of 1923*. It was the first Hemingway story to appear in hard cover. Hadley had more good news: She was pregnant.

Tiring of Rapallo, the couple moved to the Alpine town of Cortina in northern Italy, where Hemingway spent his time writing and skiing. Here he produced "Out of Season," the story of a couple on a fishing trip in Italy and their unscrupulous guide. The piece was more sophisticated than his earlier prose.

In June of 1923, together with several friends, Hemingway made his first trip to Spain to watch the bullfights. He enjoyed the country so much that he returned the following month with Hadley to see (and participate in) the famous "running of the bulls" in Pamplona. He developed a deep and lifelong respect for the matadors who bravely faced death each time they walked into the ring.

One of Hemingway's companions on that first trip to Spain, publisher Robert McAlmon, decided to publish *Three Stories and Ten Poems* (1923), Hemingway's first collection of short stories. The book contained the stories "Up in Michigan," "My Old Man" and "Out of Season" plus poetry.

The Hemingways returned to Toronto in the fall of 1923 and Hadley delivered a boy, John Hadley Nicanor (Nicanor Villalta was a bullfighter Hemingway admired), nicknamed Bumby. Meanwhile, back in Paris, some of Hemingway's fictional sketches were being compiled by another publisher friend. This book was entitled *in our time*, and only a couple of hundred copies were printed. (*in our time* is not to be confused with the 1925 *In Our Time*, Hemingway's first book published in America. The former is a small collection of brief sketches; the latter is a collection of full-length short stories, with the sketches used as interchapters.)

The Hemingways returned to Paris in January of 1924, and Ernest began writing short stories about a youth in the woods of northern Michigan and the battlefields of France. Named Nick Adams, he was one of Hemingway's earliest autobiographical characters. Hemingway's friends encouraged him to send these new stories to an American publisher. With the help of his old friend Sherwood Anderson, the manuscript found its way to the editorial desk of Boni & Liveright in New York.

In the meantime, his *Three Stories and Ten Poems* had been noticed by the esteemed American critic Edmund Wilson, who said that Hemingway's stories had "more artistic dignity" than any American fiction to come out of the war period. Hemingway then received the happy news that Boni & Liveright had accepted *In Our Time*.

Hemingway's reputation as a new voice in American fiction was now beginning to grow. Another American expatriate writer of the day, F. Scott Fitzgerald, was so impressed with Hemingway's fiction that he recommended it to Max Perkins, his editor at Scribner's. Perkins wrote Hemingway a letter offering to consider publishing his next book. Hemingway had the chance to thank Fitzgerald in person when they finally met in a Parisian bar in May of 1925.

Hemingway was both envious of and impressed by Fitzgerald's Princetonian charm and runaway success as a writer; Fitzgerald admired Hemingway's raw masculinity and the clarity of his prose. The two became friends, but in later years, as Fitzgerald's popularity slipped, the tide would turn, and it would be Hemingway who would command the respect and envy of Fitzgerald.

Hemingway now felt the time was ripe for a longer work and began to gather the material for his first novel. Based on his own European experiences, *The Sun Also Rises* (1926) is the story of shallow romance and betrayal between friends on a trip from Paris to Spain. Hemingway explored the aimlessness of his characters' lives, many of them based on the lives of real people. When the book was released, he got into more than a few arguments with friends who didn't enjoy being publicly disgraced in the pages of his fiction. Yet, as with Fitzgerald's *This Side of Paradise*, the book became immensely popular among American college students, who tried to mimic the novel's colorful characters such as Lady Brett Ashley or the hard-boiled Jake Barnes.

Hemingway followed up *In Our Time* with *Torrents of Spring* (1926)—a scathing parody of Sherwood Anderson's work. He wrote *Torrents* because he was tired of being compared to and associated with his former mentor. The book severed his relationship not only with Anderson but with Boni & Liveright as well, and Hemingway walked into the waiting arms of Maxwell Perkins at Scribner's—Hemingway's publisher for the rest of his life.

The release of *Torrents* was followed by *The Sun Also Rises*, and Hemingway was on his way to permanent popularity as a writer. He began writing stories for *Scribner's Magazine* and working on a new collection of short fiction, *Men Without Women* (1927).

Comprised of fiction that lacks, as Hemingway put it, "the softening feminine influence," *Men Without Women* contains stories of his experiences in Michigan, Spain and wartime Italy. The best of Hemingway's short fiction can be found here, together with *In Our Time*. Although some reviewers, such as Virginia Woolf, found *Men Without Women* "too self consciously virile," it was immensely popular, selling 15,000 copies in the first three months.

Hemingway's personal life was taking some turns as well. He divorced Hadley in January of 1927 to take up with Pauline Pfeiffer, a young Arkansas heiress and reporter for the Paris edition of *Vogue*, whom he had met the previous year. He married Pauline in May, and by the following fall she was pregnant. After a trip to Arkansas to visit her parents, the Hemingways went on to Kansas City, where Pauline gave birth to a boy, Patrick. To get a little peace and quiet, Hemingway went off to Wyoming on a fishing trip and continued to work on *A Farewell to Arms*, which he had begun writing before he left Paris.

That winter the whole family rented a house in Key West, Florida, where Hemingway had spent six happy weeks in the fall. He and the family were on their way to the Keys when Hemingway received the news that his father had died. When he got to Oak Park he was shocked to learn that the death had been caused by suicide. He himself had an obsession with suicide, and the thought of taking his own life haunted him the rest of his days.

The family spent the spring of 1929 in Paris and the summer in Spain, where Hemingway was gathering material for *Death in the Afternoon* (1932), a book about bullfighting. *A Farewell to Arms*—considered to be one of Hemingway's finest works and one of the best war novels of the era—was published on Hemingway's return to Paris, and the reviews were more than good. The purity and simple beauty of the book's opening lines demonstrate how far the author had come in search of his "one true sentence."

In the late summer of that year we lived in a house in a village that looked across the river and the plain to the mountains. In the bed of the river there were pebbles and boulders, dry and white in the sun, and the water was clear and swiftly moving and blue in the channels. Troops went by the house and down the road and the dust they raised powdered the leaves of the trees.

Hemingway drew heavily on his war experiences for the plot. It is the story of a love affair between Frederic Henry, a wounded World War I American lieutenant in the Italian ambulance service, and Catherine Barkley, an English nurse. Catherine becomes pregnant and Henry deserts to run away with her to Switzerland after Italy's horrible defeat at Caporetto. Catherine dies in childbirth, and Henry is left in a shattered world, questioning the dignity of human life and the absurdity of war.

The book was praised for its depictions of war, especially the account of the Italian army's painful retreat from the battlefield. The novel was also considered in bad taste by some (it was banned, for instance, in Boston) because of its use of obscene language and graphic passages such as the following:

I loved to take her hair down and she sat on the bed and kept very still, except suddenly she would dip down to kiss me while I was doing it, and I would take out the pins and lay them on the sheet and it would be loose and I would watch her while she kept very still and then take out the last two pins and it would all come down and she would drop her head and we would both be inside of it . . .

Basking in his success, Hemingway now entered a new phase in his career. No longer the young and struggling unknown writer, he enthusiastically embraced the new image of himself—that of "Papa" Hemingway, the seasoned, sporting, lusty author.

Pauline added another son, Gregory, to the Hemingway family in the fall of 1931, and her uncle bought a house for them all in Key West. Hemingway flourished here, making Key West his new Paris. It was here that he was introduced to the sport of marlin fishing, which became a life-long passion, and it was at a local bar called Sloppy Joe's that he became a regular and legendary patron. He and Pauline often took day-long trips to Cuba, where Hemingway fished and worked on stories for *Cosmopolitan* and *Scribner's* magazines. Some of these ended up in his next collection of short stories, *Winner Take Nothing* (1933), which, aside from the story "A Clean Well-Lighted Place," was a critical disappointment. He also wrote his first piece of feature journalism in ten years—a story about game fishing—for a new men's magazine called *Esquire*, with which he developed a longtime publishing relationship.

Death in the Afternoon was generally panned by the critics for being too macho, too puffed up with male bravado. Hemingway despaired over the reviews (which he always took personally) but got right to work on his third novel, *To Have and Have Not* (1937), based on his Cuban experiences. It is the story of Harry Morgan, a Key West native and family man who runs a fishing boat. When times get hard during the Depression, he turns to smuggling and rum-running to support his family but is shot and killed helping a gang of escaping bank robbers. Harry's dying words, "One man alone ain't got . . . no chance," reflect Hemingway's sympathy for the cast-off, struggling victims of the Depression.

In the fall of 1933, Hemingway fulfilled a personal fantasy by setting out for East Africa on a hunting safari, with Pauline and some friends. His experiences there and on safari resulted in several stories, notably "The Snows of Kilamanjaro" and "The Short Happy Life of Francis Macomber." He also turned his journal of the trip into his second work of nonfiction, *The Green Hills of Africa* (1935).

Back in Key West, Hemingway resumed his routine of writing in the mornings and fishing in the afternoons off Cuba and Bimini aboard his new 38-foot, twin-engine powerboat, the *Pilar*. Meanwhile, bad reviews of *The Green Hills of Africa* reflected the public's (or at least the critics') increasing ambivalence over "Papa" Hemingway.

"Papa" Hemingway, the seasoned author on his second safari to Kenya in 1953. Hemingway was an enthusiastic sportsman all his life and took delight in burnishing his own popular image as a macho man. In the end, he would turn a rifle on himself and commit suicide.
(Hemingway Collection, John F. Kennedy Library)

In December of 1936, at Sloppy Joe's, he met a young, attractive blonde-haired journalist named Martha Gellhorn. Educated at Bryn Mawr, a published novelist as well as a journalist, Gellhorn told Hemingway that she planned to go to Europe to cover the Spanish Civil War.

Hemingway left for Spain himself in March of 1937 as a correspondent for the North American Newspaper Alliance and to take part in the making of a documentary film about the war called *The*

Spanish Earth. Martha Gellhorn arrived in Spain soon after, on assignment for *Colliers* magazine, and within a month she and Hemingway were having an affair. Some of Hemingway's correspondent friends observed that Martha, unlike others in "Papa"'s circle, was refreshingly independent and didn't behave like a courtier in his presence.

Hemingway returned to the Keys in May for more fishing off Bimini while, again, another Hemingway book—*To Have and Have Not*—got mixed reviews. Many critics felt that the book's theme of social consciousness was poorly crafted. Some hinted that Hemingway's style was becoming dated and that his view of life was too narrow. Nevertheless, the public still seemed to enjoy his work, and the book was a best-seller within a month.

Hemingway thought he might try his hand at drama next. *The Fifth Column* (1938) was a play about a manly foreign correspondent (bearing a strong resemblance to Hemingway) involved with spies and intrigue during the Spanish Civil War. The lady correspondent of the play, Dorothy Bridges, was blonde and well-educated and obviously based on Martha Gellhorn.

As Europe seemed to be moving closer to war, Hemingway couldn't resist the urge to return there, and he and Pauline left for Paris in March of 1938. With the fall of the Loyalist forces in Spain in March of 1939, the civil war was over. Hemingway said, the "hell with war for a while, I want to write."

Between his Cuban trips and his recent war adventures he had amassed a vast amount of material, which he began converting into stories for *Esquire* and *Cosmopolitan*. He had a few longer works in mind as well, including one about an old Cuban fisherman who spends several days and nights alone in his skiff combating a huge marlin, only to lose it to sharks.

But first, Hemingway got to work on a new novel based on his war experiences in Spain. By April of 1940 he was done, and was busy sifting through the pages of Shakespeare and the Bible for a title. He eventually found a quote from the English poet John Donne, which summed up the theme of his new book:

> . . . *any man's death diminishes me, because I am involved in Mankinde; and therefore never send to know for whom the bell tolls; it tolls for thee.*

For Whom the Bell Tolls (1940) is considered one of Hemingway's most ambitious novels. An American college professor, Robert Jordan, goes to Spain during the civil war to fight for the Republican army. He is attached to a band of guerrillas and is given the task of blowing up a strategic bridge. He falls in love with a peasant girl, Maria, who has been raped by the fascists, but their brief affair is marred by troubles among the guerrillas, who mistrust their leaders. Jordan blows up the bridge but is wounded and left to die.

In *For Whom the Bell Tolls*, Hemingway gives us a loving portrayal of a country and people he admired, plus an examination of a complicated war in which elevated, ideological passions are contrasted with destruction and brutality.

The novel's success lies in its timelessness, which Hemingway achieved by keeping the focus on the bridge and its destruction. "[T]hat bridge can be the point on which the future of the human race can turn," he wrote in *For Whom the Bell Tolls*. The symbolism goes beyond the fate of his characters: Blowing up the bridge means assurance of a world free from fascists.

The death of Robert Jordan represents the tragic deaths of thousands who struggled for freedom and independence in the Spanish Civil War and all wars. As Jordan lies on the hillside above the bridge in his final moments, the significance of the Donne quote ("No man is an Iland, intire of itselfe . . .") becomes clear; even the earth feels the passage of this one human life:

He was completely integrated now and then he took a good long look at everything. Then he looked up at the sky. There were big white clouds in it. He touched the palm of his hand against the pine needles where he lay and he touched the bark of the pine trunk that he lay behind.

The critics and the public reacted positively to Hemingway's latest achievement. It was a Book-of-the-Month Club selection, and the film rights sold for an unprecedented $100,000. It was nominated for the 1941 Pulitzer Prize in literature but was ultimately rejected because of its controversial sex scenes and political themes.

Even though he didn't get the Pulitzer this time, *For Whom the Bell Tolls*, like *A Farewell to Arms*, represented a turning point in Hemingway's life. It was one of the last major efforts of his career, although at the time he didn't realize it. Edging toward the ripeness of his middle age, but bloated by his own increasingly fictionalized reputation, the legendary "Papa" Hemingway was gradually becoming less of a writer and more of a public figure.

His personal life was also undergoing changes. As his relationship with Pauline deteriorated, he spent more time out on the *Pilar* or in Havana. He was finally joined in Cuba by Martha Gellhorn, who found a house for them both on an old estate called *Finca Vigía*. She had the place fixed up and Hemingway moved in with her. He finally divorced Pauline and in the fall of 1940 asked Martha to join him at Sun Valley, a new hunting spot he had discovered in Central Idaho. They were married there.

Soon after the wedding, *Collier's* sent Martha off to cover the war being fought by Chinese leader Chiang Kai-shek against aggressive Japanese invaders. Hemingway lined up some assignments for himself and accompanied Martha to the Far East in January of 1941. Feeling upstaged by his wife, Hemingway was grumpy most of the time and returned to the United States early.

He had more to groan about at home. Critic Edmund Wilson, who once had praise for Hemingway, was now claiming that the author's "[c]raftsmanship and style, taste and sense" had all but disappeared. Wilson upbraided Hemingway for his arrogance and publicity-seeking, claiming that "the heroic Hemingway legend [had] . . . invaded his fiction." Wilson also observed Hemingway's "growing antagonism to women"—a criticism that persists to this day.

Hemingway, like the rest of America, was shocked to hear about the Japanese attack on Pearl Harbor in December of 1941. With the United States entering World War II, Hemingway was ready to do his part. He used the *Pilar* as an espionage vessel, scouring the waters of the Caribbean for Nazi submarines, before going to Europe to cover the war for *Collier's*.

While in Europe, he met and fell in love with a 36-year-old, blonde journalist in *Life* magazine's London bureau, Mary Welsh Monks. Although Mary was married herself, she fell under Papa's spell, and the two wrote to each other while Hemingway was on the Continent. They had an affair, and he finally divorced Martha. Mary agreed to divorce her husband and join Hemingway back at the *Finca Vigía* in Cuba, where he returned in April of 1945. They were married a year later, and Mary settled into the *Finca* as the fourth and final Mrs. Hemingway.

The author got back to work on his fiction, producing 1,000 pages of a new novel, *The Garden of Eden*, a strange book based on his earlier marriages and life in Europe during the twenties.

He never actually finished the novel and worked at it, off and on, until his death. Scribner's published it posthumously in 1986.

In the fall of 1948, Hemingway took Mary with him on a tour of Italy to relive the glory of his days in the First World War. During the trip he worked on *Across the River and into the Trees* (1950), the story of a World War I veteran revisiting the sites of his war days. The book was considered inferior by most critics but was nonetheless popular with the reading public.

Hemingway still took criticism very personally, and Mary was beginning to see the other side of Papa—the childish, irritable, foul-mouthed bear of a man who insulted people and flew into tantrums. Aside from his easily bruised ego, Hemingway was also suffering from physical ailments, which included a swollen leg (possibly due to a piece of shrapnel left from his war wound) and high blood pressure. His doctors advised him to lose some weight and he had to go on a diet, which darkened his mood.

But the act of writing lifted his spirits, and from 1950 to 1951 he worked on the story he had heard about an old Cuban fisherman who catches a magnificent marlin. The old man of Hemingway's story, Santiago, "had gone for eighty-four days . . . without taking a fish," and is considered unlucky. But his faithful companion, the boy Manolin, believes in him and wishes Santiago "[g]ood luck" as the old man "left the smell of the land behind and rowed out into the clean early morning smell of the ocean."

Santiago eventually hooks a 1,000-pound marlin—"the biggest fish that he had ever seen and bigger than he had ever heard of"—and his struggle to land the creature becomes a two-day, pitched battle in which he must rely on all his skill and resources just to stay alive. The marlin finally dies, but Santiago's battle continues as he fights off ravenous sharks, who pick the magnificent carcass clean by the time the skiff returns to the harbor. The old man nobly accepts what has happened, knowing that he put up an admirable fight. Hemingway ends his story with a bitter note of irony as a couple of tourists mistake the skeleton of the marlin for that of a shark.

The Old Man and the Sea (1952) won Hemingway the Pulitzer Prize he was denied in 1941. It is one of his most widely read and respected novels. Santiago's experience has been interpreted as man's struggle with his own existence and mortality; although he inevitably loses his prize catch to the sharks, the old man maintains his dignity and courage in the face of certain failure.

Some have seen Santiago's battle as symbolic of Hemingway's own duel with encroaching disillusionment and doubts about himself as a writer and his place in the world. When the old man sleeps, he dreams scenes from his youth—of lions "playing like young cats" on an African beach. Like Santiago, Hemingway often retreated to the safety of the past when he feared that his accomplishments would come to nothing.

Africa was a part of that past, and so in June of 1953 the Hemingways set off for Kenya on safari. The trip lasted for several months, and Hemingway happily bagged his share of lion, rhino and kudu.

Back home in Cuba in the fall of 1954, he learned that he was the recipient of that year's Nobel Prize for literature. He chose not to attend the ceremony in Sweden but sent along a note of gratitude, part of which read: "For a true writer each book should be a new beginning where he tries again for something that is beyond attainment. He should always try for something that has never been done or that others have tried and failed. Then, sometimes with luck, he will succeed."

All his life Hemingway tried to outdo others—other writers, other sportsmen, even himself. This determination, coupled with a bit of the luck he referred to, had made him probably the most popular writer in America at that time. But his lust for life had left him, at age 60, in poor mental and physical shape. He was having trouble finishing *The Garden of Eden*, and this angered and frightened him. In addition, his poor diet and alcohol consumption, coupled with his restless life-style, were all catching up with him. He was becoming, in the words of biographer Carlos Baker in *Ernest Hemingway: A Life Story*, "no more than a shadow of his former self."

He needed to slow down. With the Cuban revolution heating up, he was forced to leave his beloved *Finca* and head for the cool tranquility of the western mountains. He rented a house in Ketchum, Idaho, where the game hunting was good, and he tried to get back to work. He and Mary enjoyed Ketchum so much that they bought a house there in the spring of 1959.

On a trip to Spain in 1960, it was becoming clear that Hemingway was teetering on the edge of a breakdown. He fretted about his house in Havana and his income taxes. He believed the FBI was trailing him and had bugged his house and phone. He exploded at a waiter in a restaurant in Madrid for no apparent reason and suspected that his friends were trying to kill him. In addition, he was suffering from nightmares, memory loss and painful cramps in the area of his kidneys.

Back in the United States, he checked into the Mayo Clinic in Rochester, Minnesota, for observation. In addition to depression, doctors there diagnosed hypertension, diabetes and an enlarged liver from excessive alcohol consumption. He stayed in Rochester for a couple of months, returning to Ketchum in January of 1961.

It was often painful for Mary Hemingway to be with her husband now. "Ernest wanted no visitors," she wrote in her memoir, *How It Was*. "[H]e spent his mornings mute and brooding at his writing table, his afternoons wandering aimlessly around the house or resting without reading in his room." In February, Hemingway received a request to contribute a sentence or two to a book of individual tributes to President Kennedy. He sat down after lunch to work on the job; by supper time Mary found him still "hunched over the desk," unable to write a word.

One morning, she came downstairs to find Hemingway standing in front of a window with a shotgun in his hand and two shells ready on the window sill. She sat down on the sofa and talked to him gently about his accomplishments, remaining calm for an eternal 50 minutes until the doctor arrived for his regular visit. He coaxed Hemingway into handing over the gun and arranged to have his patient sent back to Rochester.

The doctors were convinced after a month that Hemingway was sane, but Mary had serious doubts. Reluctantly, she returned with him to Ketchum on Friday, June 30. Early the following Sunday morning, she woke to "the sound of a couple of drawers banging shut." When she came downstairs, she saw "a crumpled heap of bathrobe and blood." Even though the guns in the house had been locked away, Hemingway knew where the key was hidden. He had taken a shotgun, placed the twin barrels against his forehead and pulled the triggers.

In the years following his death, Hemingway, the "biggest lion" of his generation, would endure a good number of "posthumous assaults on his reputation," in the words of critic Malcolm Cowley in his essay, "Mr. Papa." Many critics found the macho posturing of Hemingway's prose distasteful and intrusive. His treatment of women, they said, was inadequate at best and abusive at worst. Aside from *The Sun Also Rises, For Whom the Bell Tolls* and a handful of the early short stories, the importance of his fiction was diminished by critics who declared that Hemingway wasn't skilled enough to produce a novel of lasting value.

The pendulum has swung back in recent decades, and Hemingway remains required reading at many high schools and in college survey courses in American literature. Even at the time of these "posthumous assaults," critics like Malcolm Cowley believed that Hemingway's work was "clearly permanent" and that American literature is "vastly richer now than it was when Hemingway started writing."

For all his faults, Hemingway was still a "highly original talent," as Baker puts it, who "spawned imitators by the score and dealt, almost single-handed, a permanent blow against the affected, the namby-pamby, the pretentious and the false."

Whether one likes Hemingway or not, there is no denying that he played an essential role in shaping modern American fiction. Beneath the trademark simplicity of his prose and the masterful dialogue lurk profound truths about the nature of violence and conflict in our society and humankind's need to understand the nature of its existence. He is also noteworthy for his exploration of human relationships and of the many emotions, such as jealousy, love and desire, that accompany them.

In a 1954 interview, *Paris Review* editor George Plimpton asked Hemingway what he thought was the "function" of his art. The writer replied, in part, that "you make something through your own invention that is not a representation, but a whole new thing truer than anything true and alive . . . and if you make it well enough, you will give it immortality. That is why you write and for no other reason."

Chronology

July 21, 1899 born in Oak Park, Illinois

1917 graduates from Oak Park High School, gets reporter's job on the *Kansas City Star*

1918 drives an ambulance during World War I; is wounded in Italy

1921 marries Hadley Richardson; moves to Paris

1923 first trip to Spain; *Three Stories and Ten Poems*, first published book

1926 *Torrents of Spring*; *The Sun Also Rises*

1927–28 divorces Hadley; marries Pauline Pfeiffer and moves to Key West

1929 *A Farewell to Arms*, first major commercial success

1933–39 first safari in Africa; *Green Hills of Africa* (1935); moves to Cuba

1940 divorces Pauline, marries Martha Gellhorn; *For Whom the Bell Tolls*

1945 divorces Martha, marries Mary Welsh Monks

1952 *The Old Man and the Sea* wins Pulitzer Prize

July 2, 1961 commits suicide at his home in Ketchum, Idaho

Further Reading

Hemingway's Works

A Farewell to Arms (New York: Charles Scribner's Sons, 1929). Hemingway's novel of wartime romance that shook the reading public.

For Whom the Bell Tolls (New York: Charles Scribner's Sons, 1940). The Spanish Civil War provides the setting for one of Hemingway's best novels.

The Old Man and the Sea (New York: Charles Scribner's Sons, 1980). A reissue of Hemingway's Pulitzer Prize–winning novel, with an introduction by Charles Scribner Jr. and striking illustrations.

The Complete Short Stories of Ernest Hemingway (New York: Charles Scribner's Sons, 1987).

Books About Hemingway

Carlos Baker, *Ernest Hemingway: A Life* (New York: Macmillan, 1969). Substantial adult biography, recognized as the definitive work on the writer's life.

Matthew J. Bruccoli, editor, *Conversations with Ernest Hemingway* (Jackson: University Press of Mississippi, 1986). A collection of interviews with and news stories about Ernest Hemingway, from the time he returned from World War I in 1919 up to the year before his death; includes many candid remarks and personal insights.

Matthew J. Bruccoli, *Scott and Ernest* (Carbondale and Edwardsville: Southern Illinois University Press, 1978). Evenhanded, critical study of one of the most famous literary friendships of all time.

Anthony Burgess, *Ernest Hemingway and His World* (New York: Charles Scribner's Sons, 1985). A concise biography that attempts to "disentangle [Hemingway's] personality from [his] persona." Lavishly illustrated with many rare photographs of Hemingway and some major people and places in his life, such as Fitzgerald, James Joyce, Maxwell Perkins and Paris in the twenties.

Peter L. Hays, *Ernest Hemingway* (New York: Continuum, 1990). A brief but good biography of the author.

Earl Rovit and Gerry Brenner, editors, *Ernest Hemingway* (Boston: Twayne, 1986). A good introduction to the life and work of Ernest Hemingway. Part of Twayne's United States Author series.

John Steinbeck
(1902–1968)

John Steinbeck in a publicity photo taken for the publication of Cannery Row. *In between semesters at Stanford University, the northern California native worked as a ranch-hand, and it was in the bunkhouses and the fields that he met the models for many of his fictional characters.*
(National Archives)

*J*ohn Steinbeck was on his way to San Francisco when he stopped off at a hobo camp for a night's rest and some company. It was during the early 1920s, and the young laborer and ranch hand who would eventually win both the Pulitzer and Nobel prizes in literature was bumming around his native northern California in search of stories.

He asked the men at the camp—mostly World War I veterans down on their luck—if they had any tales to share. He heard a few good jokes but said that he was after something more "humanistic." Then one man came forward and related how he had been lost for days in a huge thicket of canes on the Oregon coast. Weakened by thirst and hunger, he finally found his way to the door of a nearby farmhouse and collapsed. As the man lay dying, too feeble to eat, the farmer convinced his wife, who was nursing a baby, to feed the stranger from her breast. The act saved his life.

Steinbeck listened to this story and then paid the man two dollars, saying, "Thanks. I can use that."

And use it he did, in the powerful and controversial ending of his masterpiece, *The Grapes of Wrath* (1939). This was just one of the many hundreds of stories and experiences John Steinbeck wove into the rich tapestry of his fiction. Always keeping his eyes and ears open for details, he produced novels, short stories, newspaper articles and journals—many of them set against the backdrop of the Salinas Valley in California.

Although he achieved worldwide fame and is now ranked with Faulkner and Hemingway as one of American literature's preeminent writers, Steinbeck always felt more comfortable and found more inspiration in simply chatting with the man down at the hardware store or talking with a struggling migrant worker and his family. As Ma Joad, a central character in *The Grapes of Wrath*, puts it: "If you're in trouble or hurt or need—go to poor people. They're the only ones that'll help—the only ones."

John Ernst Steinbeck knew what it was to be poor himself. He was born on February 27, 1902, and grew up in the small, rural town of Salinas, California, near the dramatic Monterey coast. His father was a man of modest means who ran a feed store, and his mother was a school teacher.

Owing to his mother's influence, young Steinbeck was fond of reading, especially Greek myths and the tales of King Arthur in Sir Thomas Malory's *Morte d'Arthur*. In his earliest experiences as a storyteller, he drew on these works to entertain his friends with fairy tales and ghost stories.

A lazy and stubborn youth who did just enough work to get the grades his parents expected of him, Steinbeck was nevertheless considered a prize pupil by his composition teachers, who often read his work aloud in class. This praise made him decide to be a writer, and upon graduation from high school in 1919 he entered Stanford University to pursue a degree in English with an emphasis on creative writing and journalism.

Steinbeck's career in higher education was spotty. Ignoring Stanford's set curriculum, he took whatever courses interested him (many of which, oddly enough for an English major, were in the biological sciences), and his record is peppered with incompletes. He also developed a pattern of attending school for a term and then taking time off to work on the ranches in the Salinas Valley.

It was here, in the fields and the bunkhouses, that he encountered the models for many of his fictional characters. Lennie and George in *Of Mice and Men* (1937) and the *paisanos* with their colorful stories of *Tortilla Flat* (1935) were drawn from the drifters and the Mexican laborers with whom Steinbeck worked.

In 1925 he gave up the idea of getting his degree and headed to New York City to become a writer. He got work on a construction crew building a new Madison Square Garden but hated the work and appealed to a rich uncle, who was able to get him a reporter's job on the New York *American*. Since Steinbeck was actually more of a storyteller than a journalist, the job didn't last long. After he was let go, he boasted that he finally had the credentials he needed to be a writer—he had been fired by a Hearst paper.

During this time he had also been busy writing short stories, a form he always felt most comfortable with. He worked feverishly to put together a story collection after a junior editor at Robert McBride expressed interest in his work. When he returned weeks later, the editor had moved on. The man who had taken his place didn't want even to look at the manuscript. After Steinbeck threatened to tear him limb from limb, he had the enraged young writer tossed out onto the street.

Broke and dejected, Steinbeck had no choice but to head back to California, where he took a job as the caretaker of an estate on Lake Tahoe. Holed up for the winter in a little caretaker's cabin at the abandoned summer resort, he continued to work on his fiction. In the spring of 1926 he published his first short story, "The Gifts of Iban," in a new magazine called *The Smokers Companion*.

The story was labeled "a fantasy" and takes place in an enchanted forest, with fairies and other such characters drawn from Steinbeck's fascination with Malory. His first novel, *The Cup of Gold* (published, ironically, by Robert McBride), was also a fantasy, based on the life of the buccaneer Sir Henry Morgan. Steinbeck's creative process often followed this pattern: He would sketch out central themes and characters in his short fiction, giving them more depth in longer works. Many episodes and even passages of dialogue in *The Grapes of Wrath*, *Tortilla Flat* or *The Winter of Our Discontent* can be found in Steinbeck's earlier short fiction.*

Steinbeck lost his caretaker job after a fallen tree caved in the roof of the estate house, and he moved on to San Francisco. In 1930 *The Cup of Gold* was published, and Steinbeck married Carol Henning, a woman he had been dating in San Francisco. The couple moved into a house in Pacific Grove, where the writer worked on his second novel, *To a God Unknown* (1933). Set in the Salinas Valley, the book is notable for being Steinbeck's first piece of "local color." It was followed by *The Pastures of Heaven* (1932) which was about the lives of the residents in a California town of that name.

As he began to focus on what he was most familiar with—the agrarian valleys of northern California and the lives of the people there—his fiction grew richer and more accomplished. Jody and Billy Buck in *The Red Pony* (1933) and Elisa Allen in the short story "Chrysanthemums," are examples of characters whom Steinbeck knew from personal experience. His sensitivity to their real-life situations made his stories more involving and moving.

Despite his progress as a writer, the years between 1930 and 1935 were tough ones. His books didn't sell well, and barely brought in any money. One promising development during this period was his alliance with the new literary agency of McIntosh and Otis, which represented the author for the rest of his life. Another was the beginning of his close friendship with marine biologist Ed Ricketts.

Ricketts ran a lab in a fishing village on the Monterey coast. The village later became the setting for *Cannery Row* (1945). Steinbeck passed many of his afternoons down at the lab chatting with the philosophical, easygoing scientist or collecting specimens with him along the rocky coastline. Ricketts would appear in *Cannery Row* as "Doc," and many of the book's other colorful characters were based on actual residents of the village.

Steinbeck's fortunes began to turn when he sold the first two parts of *The Red Pony* plus a number of other stories to *The North American Review* in 1933. A year later, he won an O. Henry prize for his story "The Murder." He was also at work on a new novel, which he called *Tortilla Flat*.

---

* For example, compare Steinbeck's story "Breakfast" (from *The Long Valley*) with chapter 22 of *The Grapes of Wrath*.

John Steinbeck

Based on stories he picked up from Mexican fieldhands and masterfully recast as a modern-day legend of the Round Table, *Tortilla Flat* is the story of Danny, Pilon and the rest of the lazy but heroic *paisanos* who spend their days avoiding work and their nights gathered around gallon jugs of cheap wine. Of all Steinbeck's characters, the wily and conniving Pilon is among the most memorable for his ability to twist the truth into fiction and vice versa:

> *Pilon wandered into the weed-tangled back yard. Fruit trees were there, bony and black with age, and gnarled and broken from neglect. A few tent-like chicken coops lay among the weeds, a pile of rusty barrel hoops, a heap of ashes and a sodden mattress. Pilon looked over the fence to Mrs. Morales' chicken yard, and after a moment of consideration he opened a few small holes in the fence for the hens. "They will like to make nests in the tall weeds," he thought kindly.*

It was late in 1934 when Steinbeck got the biggest break of his career. *Cup of Gold* and *The Pastures of Heaven* had been recommended to publisher Pascal (Pat) Covici of Covici-Friede by a Chicago bookseller Steinbeck didn't even know. Covici admired Steinbeck's work and immediately offered him a contract. The publication of *Tortilla Flat*, and the subsequent sale of the movie rights, brought Steinbeck fame and fortune. He wasn't quite ready for all the attention—throughout his life he hated to be interviewed—but the financial success was a relief for him and Carol, after several hard years of struggle.

It was often his habit to work on several books or projects at once. While he had been busy writing *Tortilla Flat*, he had also been keeping an eye on the unrest brewing among California farmworkers. Unreasonably low wages and abusive treatment by growers were causing strikes. Labor leaders who organized the strikes were targeted as troublemakers, Communists, "Reds."

Steinbeck could see that the pot was about to boil over on this situation. He met several times with labor leaders Pat Chambers and Cicil McKiddy and decided that their stories were worth telling. The account of their struggle for justice for California fruit pickers inspired Steinbeck's first great social novel, *In Dubious Battle* (1936), in which Chambers and McKiddy appear as the two main characters, Jim and Mac.

Next, Steinbeck had an idea for a play, but Covici seemed to think the piece would work better as a short novel. *Of Mice and Men* is the story of two migrant workers—Lennie, the half-witted gentle giant, and George, his irritable yet devoted protector—who dream of owning their own farm someday. The dream is shattered when Lennie accidentally kills a girl who is trying to seduce him, and George must shoot his friend to keep him from being lynched. A Book-of-the-Month Club selection (thus assuring substantial sales), *Of Mice and Men* was later dramatized on stage (by Steinbeck) and made into several film and television adaptations. It remains one of Steinbeck's most popular and touching stories.

Meanwhile, his reputation as a social novelist was growing. Impressed by *In Dubious Battle*, an editor at the *San Francisco News* asked Steinbeck to write a series of articles on the plight of the migrant workers, or "Okies," who had been forced to emigrate from such midwestern Dust Bowl states as Oklahoma and Kansas in search of work in California. These people were living in deplorable conditions in "squatters' camps" or "Hoovervilles." The government was trying to help by setting up its own sanitary camps, and Steinbeck's editor sent him on the road to report on the situation. These articles were the seeds of *The Grapes of Wrath*, which Steinbeck would begin to write two years later.

He toured the camps and spoke extensively with camp manager Tom Collins, a tireless advocate for the Okie families. Steinbeck would later use numerous anecdotes from Collins's report on the government camps, and in the dedication of *The Grapes of Wrath*, he included this: ". . . To Tom who lived it."

Steinbeck had seen poverty before, but he was not prepared for the abject misery these farmers and their families were enduring. He witnessed starvation, floods, disease and, worst of all, crushed human spirits, as we see in a passage from one of the articles he did for the *News*, quoted in *The True Adventures of John Steinbeck, Writer* by Jackson J. Benson:

> Four nights ago the mother had a baby in the tent, on the dirty carpet. It was born dead, which was just as well because she could not have fed it at the breast; her own diet will not produce milk . . . The children do not even go to the willow clump any more. They squat where they are and kick a little dirt. The father is vaguely aware that there is hookworm in the mud along the river bank. He knows the children will get it on their bare feet.
>
> But he hasn't the will nor the energy to resist. Too many things have happened to him.

John Steinbeck

A migrant family of "Okies" on their way to California during the 1930s. Hundreds of poor farmers and their families were uprooted from their homes by the Depression and made the trip west, only to learn that there was no work for them. Steinbeck talked to many families such as these, and what he learned of their struggles moved him to write The Grapes of Wrath.
(Library of Congress)

Steinbeck made one more journey among the Okies with Collins. He helped to save thousands of families trapped in the rain and the mud after a devastating flood—an event he fictionalized in the closing chapters of *The Grapes of Wrath*—and with each passing day his anger and outrage at their situation grew. But it would take two years for it all to settle in his heart and mind before he could write what is generally considered to be his masterpiece.

His first impulse was to produce a biting, satirical book that attacked the wealthy landowners. "L'Affaire Lettuceberg" was the working title of what might be called the first draft of *The Grapes of Wrath*. However, when Steinbeck finished the book, he knew it wasn't worthy of the human suffering he had seen. Realizing that he needed to focus on the migrant families themselves, he chucked "L'Affaire" and started all over again. Driving himself hard from May through December of 1938, he finally delivered his 200,000-word novel to Pat Covici.

The publication of *The Grapes of Wrath* has been called "a national event," according to Pascal Covici Jr. in his biographical notes to *The Portable Steinbeck*. It was at once the crowning achievement of Steinbeck's career (it won the Pulitzer Prize in fiction that year) and an impediment, since the critics and the reading public continued to expect great, blockbuster novels of social upheaval to flow from his pen. Steinbeck was thus embittered by the reception given to the books that immediately followed *Sea of Cortez: A Leisurely Journal of Travel and Research* (1941), co-written by Ed Ricketts, based on a marine expedition Ricketts and Steinbeck made to the Gulf of California; and *The Forgotten Village* (1941), the novelization of a screenplay he had written about death and disease in a rural Mexican village.

Still, in retrospect, the greatness and significance of *The Grapes of Wrath* cannot be overlooked. It is, for one thing, a novel of vast movement. The migrants have to move from their homes, they move across the country to California, they are moved from camp to camp by the authorities. Even "the red country and part of the gray country" Steinbeck so beautifully describes in the opening lines of the book moved and "began to disappear."

Even though the Okies and their families endure great hardship, there is hope and dignity in what they have gone through, as expressed by the character Reverend Jim Casy: "ever' time they's a little step fo'ward, she may slip back a little, but she never slips clear back . . . an' that makes the whole thing right. An' that means they wasn't no waste even if it seemed like they was."

Steinbeck emphasized in *The Grapes of Wrath* that "repression works only to strengthen and knit the oppressed." This unity is summed up by Tom Joad, who is forced to flee from the authorities but assures Ma that he'll "be ever'where—wherever you look":

Wherever they's a fight so hungry people can eat, I'll be there. Wherever they's a cop beatin' up a guy, I'll be there . . . I'll be in the way guys

*yell when they're mad an'—I'll be in the way kids laugh when they're
hungry and they know supper's ready. An' when our folks eat the stuff
they raise an' live in the houses they build—why, I'll be there.*

Tom's belief that "maybe . . . a fella ain't got a soul of his own,
but on'y a piece of a big one . . ." seems to arise directly from the
philosophy of Emerson, who believed that human beings and all
living things are spiritually united by a common energy he called
the "over-soul."* In fact, Steinbeck was expressing his own philosophy, based on his studies in the biological sciences, that we
are all organically and ecologically linked. This theme, which runs
throughout his work, "would be one of the main things that
marked his work as different from that of his contemporaries,"
according to Benson.

After resting from his work on *The Grapes of Wrath*, Steinbeck
considered writing a marine biology textbook with Ed Ricketts.
He eventually abandoned the project, but the two did work together on *Sea of Cortez: A Leisurely Journal of Travel and Research*.
During the expedition to the Gulf of California for this book, it
was becoming evident that Steinbeck's relationship with Carol
was ending. She had supported him during the hard years, typing
and editing his manuscripts (Steinbeck wrote all his fiction in
longhand) and giving him constant encouragement. She began to
drink, however, and the couple often fought in public, until it
became too much for either of them to bear. He had also been
carrying on a secret affair with a singer named Gwyndolyn Congers, whom he had met in Hollywood.

In 1942, Steinbeck divorced Carol and moved to New York with
Gwyn Congers. He married her in March of the following year,
and they had their first child, Thom, in August of 1944. Their
second son, John, was born two years later.

With the coming of World War II, Steinbeck did his part for the
war effort by writing *Bombs Away: The Story of a Bomber Team*
(1942), a nonfiction work for the Air Force, and *The Moon is Down*
(1942), a novel about a German-occupied country in Europe,
written for the government intelligence agency (the Office of
Strategic Services) that eventually became the CIA. In 1943, he
wrote the screenplay for the Alfred Hitchcock film, *Lifeboat*. The
project started out as another wartime effort by Steinbeck, this
time for the Maritime Commission, but turned into a different

---

* Emerson borrowed this idea from Eastern philosophy.

film when director Hitchcock got involved. Also in 1943, Steinbeck was contracted by the New York *Herald Tribune* as a war correspondent to cover the European theater of conflict. His articles for the *Tribune* would later be collected in *Once There Was A War* (1958).

In the years just after the war, Steinbeck became increasingly critical and spiteful. He nurtured a particular resentment for Ernest Hemingway, whose work he had greatly admired at one point, but whose personality he found repulsive. He was also having difficulties in dealing with his own fame and success, in trying to keep his ego from getting the better of him.

Despite the turmoil of this period, he found it in himself to write one of his most amusing books, *Cannery Row*, a nostalgic, almost mythical fable about a group of social misfits based directly on characters he had met while hanging around Ed Ricketts's laboratory. The same year he also wrote the moving story of a Mexican fisherman who finds a pearl of tremendous value, only to have it bring him and his family tragedy and death. *The Pearl* (1945)—based on a legendary story Steinbeck had heard during his marine expedition to Mexico—blends many of the author's favorite elements: mythology, folkloric wisdom, the human struggle for happiness and the moral lesson that true contentment comes from within and not from without.

But as Steinbeck reached middle age, true happiness seemed to be eluding him. His marriage to Gwyn ended in a bitter divorce in 1948, after she told him that she hadn't loved him for years. The next blow came when Steinbeck's closest friend and confidant, Ed Ricketts, died in a car accident. Despite Steinbeck's attempts to branch out artistically, he was still being pigeonholed by the critics and the reading public, who were pressuring him to produce another great work like *The Grapes of Wrath*.

He had now entered a period of his life in which he traveled extensively: to Mexico, where he worked on a screenplay, *Viva, Zapata!* (1950), and got the inspiration for *The Wayward Bus* (1947); to Russia with photographer Robert Capa, out of which came the nonfiction work, *A Russian Journal* (1948); to Europe, where he lived for nine months and wrote articles for the French news magazine, *Figaro Littéraire*.

But Steinbeck was always at his best when he turned the focus on his own backyard, writing of the people and places that he loved. His two major projects in 1951 are good examples. First, he reached inside himself to write "About Ed Ricketts," a tribute to his dear friend, which appeared as a preface to *The Log of the Sea of Cortez*, a reissue of the narrative section from *Sea of Cortez*, the book he wrote with Ed Ricketts. Next, he reached even further back into his personal history to produce *East of Eden* (1952), a retelling of the Biblical story of Cain and Abel set against the backdrop of the Salinas Valley and Steinbeck's own family heritage.

He began research for the book early in 1948 with a trip back to California. He went to the newspaper offices of the *Salinas Californian* and read back issues dating to the turn of the century; he also interviewed old friends of the family and elder members of the community, mining them for stories, details and characters.

Then, putting the distance of a continent between him and his subject, he returned to New York and started work on the novel, composing most of it in the secluded hamlet of Siasconset on Massachusetts's Nantucket Island where he spent his summers.

East of Eden had all the sweep and breadth of *The Grapes of Wrath*, which Steinbeck's public was eager for, but an entirely different theme. Through the story of a father and his two sons—the virtuous yet vapid Aron and the rebellious Cal—Steinbeck explored the classic conflicts between good and evil, shame and pride, love and hate. When Cal discovers the horrible truth behind his mother's mysterious disappearance, he tells Aron out of anger and then seeks forgiveness from his father, Adam. Steinbeck's story stressed that the human gift of free will, expressed by the Hebrew word *timshel*, which Adam whispers on his deathbed, enables us to turn from and leave behind the sins of our past. The novel was fairly well received by the critics and was a number-one best-seller.

Seeking to shake the rigors of *East of Eden* out of his system, Steinbeck worked on speeches for politician Adlai Stevenson, who was running for president in 1952. Steinbeck also traveled to Europe writing articles for *Collier's* magazine, and produced a short novel, *Sweet Thursday* (1954), which continued the adventures of several *Cannery Row* characters. The book was made into a Rodgers and Hammerstein musical comedy, *Pipe Dreams*, a year later.

In 1955 Steinbeck bought a house in Sag Harbor on Long Island, New York, and it was there that the author spent most of his declining years. The peace and folksiness of the little town gave him pleasure, and he enjoyed whiling away his mornings chatting with locals at the coffee shop or debating the best ways to hook bluefish with the fishermen down at the docks. He memorialized Sag Harbor in one of his last major works, *The Winter of Our*

Discontent (1961), which irritated more than a few residents who saw themselves and their town depicted in the novel and didn't appreciate it.

In 1960, Steinbeck rigged up a camping truck and set out to find America in the company of a French poodle named Charley. *Travels with Charley* (1961) is his tribute to the country and the various people he met on his journey.

In 1962, Steinbeck was awarded the Nobel Prize for literature for his contributions to American letters. Yet even this great honor brought with it a measure of grief when the Nobel Prize committee was criticized in *The New York Times* and elsewhere for choosing a writer whose major work had been produced 20 years earlier.

From 1963 to 1967, Steinbeck spent more time traveling: on a good-will trip behind the Iron Curtain in eastern Europe; to Ireland in search of some of his ancestral roots; to Israel for *Newsday;* and to Southeast Asia to report on the war in Vietnam. Elaine Scott, Steinbeck's third wife, whom he married in 1950, said of her late husband in the introductory pages of *The Portable Steinbeck*, that even though he seemed to travel more than write during these years, "[he] was always writing *something*. I think perhaps you can say that first and last and always writing was his passion."

Steinbeck was working on a modernization of one of his earliest passions—Malory's *Morte d'Arthur*—when he suffered a small stroke at Sag Harbor on Memorial Day weekend, 1968. This was followed by a major heart attack in July. In mid-November he was rushed from Sag Harbor to a New York hospital. He hung on until December 20, when he lapsed into a coma and died.

Steinbeck surely deserves to be remembered for more than just *The Grapes of Wrath*. Throughout his career, he attempted numerous literary forms—drama, short fiction, novel, satire, screenplay—and succeeded in many of them. His great achievements lie not in one or two books but in his gift as a storyteller and his masterful ability to render the complexities of human passion in deceptively simple characters and situations.

While Fitzgerald may have been the spokesman for his generation, Steinbeck was the voice of the American conscience. Whether that voice boomed with the indignation of *In Dubious Battle* or chuckled with the good humor of *Cannery Row*, the spirit of its message was one of respect for all life and a pride in the enduring human capacity for survival and achievement.

Chronology

▬▬▬▬▬▬

February 27, 1902 born in Salinas, California

1920–24 attends Stanford University, writes for Stanford *Spectator;* takes semesters off to work on ranches in Salinas Valley

1925 quits college, goes to New York; works as a reporter for New York *American* but is fired after a few months

1930 first novel, *The Cup of Gold*; marries Carol Henning; meets Ed Ricketts; is taken on by McIntosh and Otis literary agency

1932–33 *To a God Unknown*; first two parts of *The Red Pony* appear in *North American Review*

1935 *Tortilla Flat*

1936 *In Dubious Battle*; visits migrant families and writes series of articles for San Francisco *News* that will become *The Grapes of Wrath*

1937 *Of Mice and Men*; first three parts of *The Red Pony* (in book form); to Europe; back in U.S., travels with migrant families, gathering more material for *The Grapes of Wrath*

1939 *The Grapes of Wrath*; Pulitzer Prize

1945 *Cannery Row*

1952 *East of Eden*; in Europe, reporting for *Collier's*

1961 *The Winter of Our Discontent*; to Europe with family; first heart failure

1962 wins Nobel Prize for Literature

December 20, 1968 dies after heart attack, New York City

Further Reading

Steinbeck's Works

John Steinbeck: Short Novels (New York: Viking, 1953). The best of Steinbeck's short novels are all here: *Tortilla Flat, The Red Pony, Cannery Row, The Moon Is Down* and *Of Mice and Men*; introduction by J. H. Jackson.

The Grapes of Wrath (New York: Viking Penguin, 1986). A reissue of the classic.

East of Eden (New York: Viking Penguin, 1986). A reissue.

The Portable Steinbeck, edited by Pascal Covici Jr. (New York: Viking, 1971). A good cross-representation of the writer's works, which includes some uncollected stories, Steinbeck's Nobel Prize acceptance speech and concise biographical notes. Informative introduction by Covici—whose father was Steinbeck's editor and close friend—provides insights.

Working Days, The Journals of The Grapes of Wrath, edited by Robert DeMott (New York: Viking, 1989). Steinbeck's own personal account of the writing of his best-known novel. Particularly helpful to the student doing an in-depth study of the work.

Books About Steinbeck

Jackson J. Benson, *The True Adventures of John Steinbeck, Writer* (New York: Viking, 1984). Adult biography that also pays considerable attention to discussing the writer's works.

Harold Bloom, editor, *John Steinbeck's The Grapes of Wrath* (New York: Chelsea House, 1988). Collection of scholarly essays on Steinbeck's masterpiece. Part of the Modern Critical Interpretations series.

Keith Ferrell, *John Steinbeck: The Voice of the Land* (New York: M. Evand, 1986). A thorough and well-researched young-adult biography; includes a bibliography.

Thomas French, editor, *Conversations with John Steinbeck* (Jackson: University Press of Mississippi, 1988). Selection of interviews with Steinbeck; provides some personal insights into his life and works.

Richard Wright
(1908–1960)

Young Richard Wright, whose first big novel, Native Son, *established him as a leading writer of the day. Wright's fiction helped pave the way for the recognition of black literature in American letters.*
(Library of Congress)

---

*I*t is unfortunate that the work of one of America's most successful and influential black writers is barely known to many people today. But perhaps Richard Wright—author of *Native Son* (1940), the critically acclaimed and unprecedented novel of black life in America—brought this obscurity upon himself. His self-imposed exile to France in the late 1940s slowly cut him off from mainstream America. More significantly, he lost touch with the ghettos and the troubled Southern slums which had inspired both his prose and his rage at the treatment of blacks in the United States.

It was a time when the "Jim Crow"* laws segregated blacks at virtually every level of society: They (especially southern blacks) were banished to the backs of buses, were not allowed to eat at the same lunch counters or even drink from the same water fountains as whites and had to sit in the "colored" balconies of movie theaters. Many were poorly educated, and substandard schools kept them that way. Blacks could not expect to rise above the lowest levels in the workplace, and their rights as citizens of this country were often abused or simply disregarded.

Despite this oppression, the family into which Richard Wright was born on September 4, 1908, outside Natchez, Mississippi, had a history of fighting for their rights. Nathaniel Wright, Richard's paternal grandfather, was a freed slave who held onto and successfully farmed the plot of land given to him by the government after the Civil War. This was at a time when it was rare for blacks to own real estate. Richard Wilson, Wright's namesake and maternal grandfather, was an escaped slave and a Civil War veteran. He waged a lifelong and fruitless battle with the federal government over his pension, which had been denied him due to a clerical error.

Young Richard Wright spent the first two years of his life on the plantation near Natchez where his father Nathan worked as a sharecropper. When his mother Ella wasn't helping on the plantation, she taught school. After a second son, Leon, came along, Ella and her two children moved in with her family, while Nathan gave up farming to become an itinerant laborer.

In 1911, Nathan moved his family to Memphis, Tennessee, where he eventually deserted them. Ella got a job in a white family's kitchen and did her best to provide for her children, but money and food were scarce. In his 1945 autobiography, *Black Boy*, Wright recalled waking up at night "to find hunger standing at my bedside, staring at me gauntly . . . twisting my empty guts until they ached."

Ella did her best to give young Richard an education, scraping together enough money in 1916 to get him off the streets—where he had fallen in with a gang—and send him to a private school. Just as he was beginning to enjoy school, Wright had to quit to care for his mother who had become ill. Desperate and poverty-

---

* "Jim Crow," a term dating back to the 18th century originally referred to black dances or jigs. By the mid-19th century, it had come to mean the segregation of blacks from whites.

stricken, Ella placed both her sons in an orphanage, hoping that they would at least be assured there of three meals a day. But life in the orphanage was no better, and Wright refused to stay.

Ella and the two boys spent the next several years living with different relatives: back with the Wilsons, who had moved to Jackson, Mississippi; with Ella's sister Maggie in Arkansas, where Wright first experienced racist terrorism when his uncle was killed by a band of white men; back once more with the Wilsons, where Richard, by now 13 and employable, pulled a knife on his grandmother, a strict Seventh Day Adventist, who tried to keep him from working on Saturdays, the Adventist Sabbath.

Wright continued to challenge his grandmother's authority in 1921 when he attended the Jim Hill Public School instead of returning to the Adventist school where she had sent him. As a 13-year-old fifth-grader, Wright was a few years behind his friends, but his teacher quickly recognized that he had talent and above-average intelligence. He read almost everything he could get his hands on—books, newspapers, detective magazines and dime novels (many of which were confiscated by Granny Wilson). By the time he got to the eighth grade he was writing stories of his own.

Wright published his first story in 1924. "The Voodoo of Hell's Half- Acre" was about a wicked man who tries to steal a widow's home away from her. Wright composed it in three days out of "sheer idleness" and then brought it to the editor of a local black paper where it was published.

No copies of "The Voodoo of Hell's Half-Acre" are known to exist today, but the typesetter for the newspaper recalled that the hero of the story was named James "Bigger" Thomas. Bigger was an actual person from Wright's neighborhood with a reputation for being tough. Years later, Wright would remember Bigger's explosive nature and use him in *Native Son* "as a literary symbol of black revolt," as Michel Fabre put it in his major biography, *The Unfinished Quest of Richard Wright*.

Wright was ninth-grade class valedictorian when he graduated from the Smith-Robinson Public School in May of 1925. This was the extent of his formal education. Still, he had dreams of "going north and writing books," of separating himself from the world of southern blacks, where he had to keep his eyes low and say "Yes sir!" and "No sir!" whenever a white man spoke.

Wright simply had too much spirit and intelligence to be this subservient. He was once fired from a job by his white boss because he didn't "laugh and talk like the other niggers." Another time a black friend cautioned him that if he wanted to stay alive in the South he had to "learn how to live in the South!"

"Dick . . . [y]ou act around white people as if you didn't know they were white. And they see it," Wright's friend explained. "When you're in front of white people, *think* before you act, *think* before you speak. Your way of doing things is all right among our people, but not for *white people*. They won't stand for it."

But Wright knew deep in his heart that he couldn't take his friend's advice.

"I was becoming aware of the thing that the Jim Crow laws had been drafted and passed to keep out of my consciousness," he wrote in *Black Boy*. "I was beginning to dream the dreams that the state had said were wrong, that the schools had said were taboo . . . upon which the penalty of death had been placed."

On the first leg of his journey north, in the fall of 1925, he returned to Memphis, where he got a job as a delivery boy. In his spare time, he began to read the works of Sherwood Anderson, Alexander Dumas, O. Henry and Sinclair Lewis.

By reading these great writers, Wright felt that he "knew what white men were feeling" and that the "vast distance separating me from the boss" had narrowed somewhat. In addition, these writers inspired him to find "new ways of looking and seeing" the world.

He decided that he could find these "new ways" in the northern city of Chicago. In the winter of 1927, Wright and his Aunt Maggie, who was also in search of a new place to settle, boarded a train bound for the "Windy City."

"I was not leaving the South to forget the South, but so that some day I might understand it . . ." he wrote in *Black Boy*.

I fled so that the numbness of my defensive living might thaw out and let me feel the pain . . . of what living in the South had meant.

Yet deep down, I knew that I could never really leave . . . for there had been slowly instilled into my personality and consciousness, black though I was, the culture of the South. So, in leaving, I was taking a part of the South to transplant in alien soil . . .

This alien soil was in a Chicago ghetto, home to some 200,000 blacks. Shunning the more popular amusements of his neighborhood—namely, drinking and gambling—Wright got a job as a clerk in the central post office. His experiences there would later provide material for his novel *Lawd Today* (a book he began writing in 1934 but that was only published posthumously, in 1963). Wright's job paid well enough for him to have his mother, brother and aunt join him in a relatively spacious four-room apartment in March of 1929.

It was around this time that Wright began to contemplate a literary life. He frequented Chicago's public library and expanded his reading list to include Marcel Proust, Stephen Crane and Dostoevski, among others. He continued to write short stories, experimenting with stream-of-consciousness black dialogue and "trying to depict the dwellers of the Black Belt," as he put it in *American Hunger* (1944), a sequel to *Black Boy*. (*American Hunger*, which deals with Wright's life from the time he arrived in Chicago until he went to New York, was originally a part of *Black Boy*. It was excerpted and published separately the year before *Black Boy* came out.)

He joined a black literary group and experienced his first brush with politics by meeting several members of the Universal Negro Improvement Association. They were enthusiastically spreading the philosophy of Marcus Garvey, a Jamaica-born black who advocated resettling American blacks in a newly created African nation. Wright "gave no credence" to the "ideology" of these so-called "Garveyites" but was nevertheless impressed with the "passionate hunger" of their beliefs.

With the stock market crash in October of 1929, Wright had his own physical hunger—plus that of his family—to think about. His hours at the post office were cut back, and by the fall of 1931 his job went the way of thousands of others during the economic blight of the Depression. He took whatever work he could get—street-cleaning, ditch-digging—and was reduced to going on public welfare, so that he and his family could eat.

Meanwhile, the rest of the country, and indeed the world, was also enduring hard times. The Depression had reached its depths by 1933, although a newly elected Democratic president, Franklin Delano Roosevelt, promised America economic recovery with his "New Deal." In Europe, militant fascists, with their oppressive, authoritarian systems of government, were seizing power in Italy, Spain, France, Germany and other countries, choking the life out of the Continent.

At the same time, support for the communist movement, which had burst onto the scene during the Russian Revolution of 1917, was gaining momentum. Based on the writings of Karl Marx, communism theoretically placed the power of government in the hands of the people. This pro-labor, anticapitalist philosophy appealed to many Depression-era workers who had lost their jobs, and the American Communist Party began to attract members. Blacks were especially enticed by the party's doctrine of equal rights.

The revolutionary social reforms of Marxism and the communist movement captivated Wright's imagination, just as they had Jack London's half a century before. In 1934, Wright joined one of the numerous left-wing literary clubs named for John Reed and began writing poetry for several communist publications. (Reed was an American journalist and intellectual who founded the Communist Labor Party and wrote *Ten Days That Shook the World*, a famous book on the Russian Revolution.)

"I Have Seen Black Hands," with its powerful cry for racial harmony, is noteworthy among these early poems, as we see in this passage, quoted in Fabre:

I am black and I have seen black hands
Raised in fists of revolt, side by side,
* with the white fists of white workers*
And some day—and it is this only which sustains me—
Some day there shall be millions and millions of them
On some red day in a burst of fists on a new horizon.

Wright's reputation as a writer now began to grow. In 1935, he was asked to attend the party-sponsored American Writer's Conference in New York, which brought together some of the most prominent writers of the day, such as Erskine Caldwell, John Dos Passos, Theodore Dreiser and Langston Hughes.

He was hired by the Federal Writers' Project, a program run by the Works Progress Administration (WPA). The WPA was part of Roosevelt's New Deal, which put writers and artists, among others, to work on civic projects. Wright also made a name for himself defending the contribution of the John Reed clubs to the communist movement, but ended up being a lone dissenter when it was voted that the clubs be dissolved. It was the first of many disagreements he would have with the party.

Wright began working on the draft of his first novel, *Cesspool* (later *Lawd Today*) in 1936. That year he also published one of his best short stories, "Big Boy Leaves Home," about a group of black youths who trespass on a white man's property and the lynching that follows. Wright said that in this story he was asking the question: "What quality of will must a Negro possess to live and die in dignity in a country that denied his humanity?"

In 1937, Wright left Chicago for New York where he became the Harlem editor of the *Daily Worker*, the Communist Party's major newspaper. It was a one-man operation and didn't pay much, but it was a step-up. He also helped to found and eventually edited the magazine *New Challenge*, a fringe publication of the party written primarily by and for blacks.

"Blueprint for Negro Writing," Wright's "most complete, coherent and profound statement . . . on Afro-American writing," in Fabre's words, appeared in the magazine in the fall. In his essay, Wright urged black writers to draw on their own culture and take pride in their ethnic background rather than try to imitate the literature of whites.

> . . . *a Negro writer must learn to view the life of a Negro living in New York's Harlem or Chicago's South Side with the consciousness that one-sixth of the earth surface belongs to the working class . . . Perspective for Negro writers will come when they have looked and brooded so hard and long upon the harsh lot of their race and compared it with the hopes and struggles of minority people everywhere that the cold facts have begun to tell them something.*

Although journalism was good training, Wright had no intention of making a career of it. He applied for a transfer to the New York branch of the Federal Writer's Project and awaited word. Meanwhile, in his free time he continued to work on his fiction, which he kept tucked in his desk drawer. He sent *Lawd Today* around to several publishers, but they all rejected it. He finally got a break at the end of 1937, when his short story, "Fire and Cloud," won $500 in a contest held by *Story* magazine. This recognition led to the publication of his first book, *Uncle Tom's Children* (1938), a collection of four novellas.

The stories—"Big Boy Leaves Home," "Down by the Riverside," "Long Black Song" and "Fire and Cloud," with "Bright and Morning Star" added in a later edition—are set in the rural South and deal with the violent tensions between blacks and whites. It was a subject that had not been explored before—from the black man's point of view. Wright's theme is one of young innocents, victimized by oppression, who achieve "adulthood through rebellion motivated by fear," as Addison Gayle observed in *Richard Wright, Ordeal of a Native Son.*

"White men killed the black and black men killed the white," muses Sarah, a black woman in "Long Black Song" who is raped by a white man and whose husband is burned to death by a white mob for taking his revenge. "White men killed the black because they could, and the black men killed the white men to keep from being killed."

Critical response to *Uncle Tom's Children* was generally positive. Ralph Ellison (author of *Invisible Man*) wrote in the communist publication *New Masses* that the book "represent[ed] one of the few instances in which an American Negro writer has successfully delineated the universals embodied in the Negro experience." *The New Republic* and *The New York Times* were horrified by the details of that experience, as well as with Wright's unflattering characterization of whites, but were nonetheless impressed. Even First Lady Eleanor Roosevelt, in her column for *The New York Post* (as quoted in Fabre), wrote that Wright's stories were so "vivid" that she "had a most unhappy time reading" them. Wright had made a strong first impression.

Wright quit his job at the *Daily Worker* after his transfer to the New York Federal Writer's Project came through in December of 1937. He now had more time for his fiction and spent most of 1938 working on his next novel, *Native Son*. That summer, armed with a batch of recommendations from academics, critics and even from Mrs. Roosevelt herself, he applied for a Guggenheim Fellowship, which he won the following year. The fellowship's $2,500 cash award went to support a year's worth of work. Also in 1939, Wright met and fell in love with two white women, Ellen Poplar and Dhima Rose Meadman.

Poplar was a bright, lively young woman, a Jew of Polish extraction and very active in the Communist Party. She met Wright after a party meeting and the two were immediately attracted to each other. Poplar's parents, however, did not approve of her becoming romantically involved with a black man. She went away for the summer to ponder her dilemma and finally made up her mind to marry Wright, but was dismayed to learn that in the meantime he had got engaged to Dhima Meadman.

Meadman, a divorcée and ballet dancer of Russian Jewish ancestry, was a more flamboyant personality than Poplar. Tall, swarthy and Egyptian-looking, she was the daughter of an actress and had the romantic air about her that one acquires from a life in the theater. Wright admired her independence and was physically attracted to her. Although still disappointed about Poplar, who he thought had rejected him, he married Dhima in August of 1939.

Wright's career changed forever in March of 1940 with the release of *Native Son*. He became "one of the great names among American novelists of the forties," according to Fabre. Biographer John A. Williams, in *The Most of Native Sons*, calls the book's publication "a turning point in American letters."

Never before had a black novelist written so accurately and movingly about the horrifying conditions under which blacks lived in America at the time. White readers were made painfully aware of the "murderous despair," as Williams puts it, that lurked in the black ghettos. Black readers recognized that the time had come for a change.

Wright's instrument of change is Bigger Thomas, a black youth who lives in a slum on the South Side of Chicago with his mother and sister. In the book's memorable opening scene, Wright establishes the family's poverty and the anger that drives Bigger Thomas when the youth kills a rat in the apartment.

Bigger's mother wants him to get a job; instead, he plots the holdup of a white man's store with members of his gang. He and gang member Gus meet on the street, and a passing plane (" 'Them white boys sure can fly,' said Gus.") inspires Bigger to reflect on the vast chasm that exists between the white world and that of blacks:

"Every time I think about it I feel like somebody's poking a red-hot iron down my throat. Goddamit, look! We live here and they live there. We black and they white. They got things and we ain't. They do things and we can't. It's just like living in jail . . . Sometimes I feel like something awful's going to happen to me," Bigger spoke with a tinge of bitter pride in his voice.

His words are prophetic. He backs out of the holdup scheme and finally takes a welfare job, chauffeuring for the Daltons, a rich white family. It is his first real exposure to the upper class. The Daltons are a liberal and progressive family, which serves only to confuse Bigger.

Most baffling is Mary Dalton who, together with her Communist Party boyfriend, Jan Erlone, tries to befriend Bigger. The two unwittingly humiliate him by making him take them to a popular black restaurant where he is seen by his friends dining in the company of white people.

Mary gets drunk and Bigger has to help her to her room when they get back to the Daltons. Mrs. Dalton (who is blind) is awakened by the noise and investigates. Bigger, realizing that it is dangerous for him, a black servant, to be caught in the bedroom of a rich white girl in the middle of the night, tries to silence Mary by putting a pillow over her face and accidentally suffocates her. He then carries her body to the basement, where he chops it up with an axe and burns it in the furnace.

As with characters in *Uncle Tom's Children*, the innocent has now become the criminal, forced into the role by outside circumstances beyond his control. Bigger accepts his "criminal destiny," as Fabre puts it, and perpetuates his crime by sending ransom notes to the Daltons. He kills once more, this time his mistress/girlfriend Bessie, who is too frightened to help him with his scheme to get money from the Daltons. An intense manhunt is on for Mary's killer, and Bigger is eventually caught.

His white lawyer, Attorney Max, is a party member, and the last third of *Native Son* is devoted to Bigger's musings on his crime and Max's defense strategy, mixed together with heavy doses of Wright's political beliefs. In the end, Bigger must face the death penalty, but he does so with a renewed sense of faith in himself and his friendship with Max and Jan, both of whom he initially mistrusted.

Critical reaction to *Native Son* was overwhelming. It was almost universally praised by both the white and the black press, who compared Wright to Dickens, Dreiser and other greats. The book sold out quickly and was a Book-of-the-Month Club selection. With this success came prosperity, and Wright was finally able to support himself and his family in comfort.

He was also able to take a honeymoon with Dhima. In April of 1940 the two went to Cuernavaca, Mexico, a pleasant village outside of Mexico City, popular with writers and the leisure class. Dhima enjoyed the luxurious life-style, but the class divisions made Wright, the Marxist, nervous and uncomfortable. After only ten days, he determined that Dhima was too shallow and bourgeois, and he left her and Mexico behind. He stopped off in the South as well as Chicago to visit friends and relatives on his way back home to New York where he renewed his relationship with Ellen Poplar. He married her in 1941, after divorcing Dhima.

When America entered World War II, Wright offered his services to both the Army's Office of War Information and the propaganda department but was rejected because of his controversial political activities. He abandoned the Communist Party (but not Marxist philosophy) because he believed it wasn't doing enough to advance the cause of civil rights and because he felt that it had lost its ideology. As far as he was concerned, the party, in its attempt to become accepted by mainstream America, had turned its back on blacks as it became just another cog in the wheel of the American political machine. He wrote about his withdrawal in his essay "I Tried to Be a Communist."

The issues of racial tension and segregation continued to trouble him. He saw evidence of these social sicknesses everywhere he went in America and was angered by the fact that as a black man, he still had to ride in the back of the bus down South.

Twelve Million Black Voices (1941)—a nonfiction, collaborative effort with photographer Edwin Rosskam that chronicled life in the slums—was one result of this anger. Another was *Black Boy*, which Wright began to write around this time. Lighter moments in Wright's life were the birth of his daughter Julia in 1942 and a collaboration with noted filmmaker Orson Welles on a stage adaptation of *Native Son*, the Broadway production of which was an enormous success.

Like *Native Son*, *Black Boy* became a Book-of-the-Month Club selection and received high praise when it was published in 1945. It was hailed as a new *Portrait of the Artist as a Young Man*, and everyone from Sinclair Lewis in the pages of *Esquire* to Lionel Trilling in *The Nation* recognized the book's power and well-crafted structure.

"*Black Boy* was forcing the American reader to consider the South from the black point of view," observes Fabre, "to understand that the social structures, the legal measures, the interracial etiquette of the country were all expressly designed to relegate the black man to a position from which it would be impossible to escape."

The popularity of *Black Boy* got Wright's picture in *Life* magazine, put him on radio talk shows, sent him on the lecture circuit and raised the asking price for his magazine articles to four figures. His influence in the literary world also grew. He was able to recommend giving a grant to another great black American writer, James Baldwin—an opportunity that launched Baldwin's career. He was a guest at the tables of university professors and lectured to conventions of educators on Afro-American literature.

Still, on the streets of New York, he was just another "nigger." He had to go to Harlem to get his hair cut because no white barber would let him into his shop. A deal to buy a Vermont farm quickly fell through when the owner discovered Wright was black. Wright and Ellen had to set up a dummy corporation just to buy a house in Greenwich Village. When the neighbors found out that Wright would be moving in, they attempted to stop him, even offering twice what he paid for the house.

Wright was fed up. Blacks were not treated so in other countries he had visited, such as Canada and France, where he had met Gertrude Stein in 1946. He decided to leave the United States and move to Paris, where he felt his dignity as a human being would be respected. It was a momentous and important decision. Wright would be cutting himself off from all he had known, all that had inspired his work in the past.

His mind was made up, however. In July of 1947 he, Ellen and Julia boarded a ship bound for France, and the Wrights began new lives as expatriates. Wright knew that he ran the risk "of being branded as Un-American," as he stated in the unpublished essay "I Choose Exile" (the article was bought by *Ebony* magazine, but

Wright in Paris, 1948. Wright had exiled himself in France the year before because he could no longer tolerate prejudice against blacks in the United States. He never returned to the U.S. and died in Paris in 1960.
(National Archives)

the editors decided not to publish it because they felt it was such a "violent critique," as Michel Fabre puts it; the quoted section here appears in Fabre's essay "Wright's Exile"), but he insisted that his motives were *not* Anti-American."

"I want the right to hold, without fear of punitive measures, an opinion with which my neighbor does not agree," he wrote, ". . . the right to travel wherever and whenever I please . . . the right to express publicly my distrust of the 'collective wisdom' of the people . . . the right to express, without fear of reprisal, my rejection of religion . . . "

These were, indeed, basic rights, ostensibly guaranteed in the Constitution and the Bill of Rights. Yet, in the aftermath of World War II, mistrust was brewing between the former allies, the United States and the Communist Party–dominated Russian Republic. This mistrust would eventually lead to the so-called "Cold War" between the two superpowers, and anyone associated with the Communist Party came under scrutiny by the federal government. Wright didn't escape this scrutiny, and the FBI kept a file on him as well as on many of his friends and colleagues.

The French had no such reservations about Wright and welcomed him with open arms. He befriended the great French writers Jean-Paul Sartre and Simone de Beauvoir, and he settled into his new European life-style. He began writing a new novel; a second daughter, Rachel, was born; and from 1948 to 1950 Wright stayed busy working on a screen adaptation of *Native Son*, in which he himself played Bigger Thomas.

Hollywood had expressed an interest in the book, but Wright wouldn't trust any of the studios there to do his story justice. Instead, he collaborated with a French producer and the movie was shot mostly in Argentina, where production costs were cheaper. Still, the project was fraught with financial as well as personnel problems. When it debuted in American movie houses, it was panned by the critics for using amateur actors, and the censors cut the film to ribbons. It was a huge flop and Wright was happy to return to things he was better suited to—writing and fighting against social injustice.

He helped to form the Franco-American Fellowship in 1950, an organization dedicated to abolishing discrimination and to helping expatriate blacks find living quarters. He became active in the *Présence Africaine*, a group that provided support to young African intellectuals caught between their native cultures and the technological civilization of the Western world.

In 1953 his new novel, *The Outsider*, was published. Partly auto-biographical, *The Outsider* is a troubling and violent story about a black man caught in a Chicago ghetto who breaks free by joining the Communist Party. He takes night classes and educates himself by reading the works of existential philosophers, then goes to New York where he impulsively murders two men. He is plagued by his conscience and hunchbacked district attorney Eli Houston. Houston lets him go for lack of evidence in the end but promises Cross that he'll "be punished," yet "not in the way" he thinks.

"I'm going to let you keep this in your heart to the end of your days," Houston tells him. "Sleep with it, eat with it, brood over it, make love with it . . . You are going to punish yourself, see? You are your own law, so you'll be your own judge . . . I wouldn't *help* you by taking you to jail."

Wright's message in the book was that society on both sides of the Iron Curtain (that is the democratic and communist worlds) existed under tyranny and was heading for a big fall.

"[T]he future of mankind will consist of . . . quite useless and reasonless suffering before any 'way out' can be found," Wright predicted, "and that when that 'way out' is found, our world, which includes America as well as Russia, will be no more."

The American critics couldn't agree with Wright and found his book hyper-violent and simply a poorly retold version of *Native Son*. Wright quickly followed *The Outsider* with *Savage Holiday* (1954), his only book with only white characters.

Wright now looked toward Africa and the Third World for inspiration. He focused his attention on the West African nation of the Gold Coast (present-day Ghana), a country in the throes of transition from colonial tribalism to independence. Wright toured the country, and the report of his visit was published under the title *Black Power* (1954).

Wright came away from his trip with a vigorous sense of pride in and awareness of his African roots, plus a heightened sensitivity to the issues of non-whites. He traveled to Bandung, Indonesia, in 1955 to cover a non-white, international conference on Third World independence. The result of his coverage was *The Color Curtain: A Report on the Bandung Conference* (1956).

He also spent time in Spain, profiling that country in the aftermath of revolution and dictatorship in *Pagan Spain: A Report of a Journey into the Past* (1956). He summed up his views on the oppression under which non-whites existed in the world in a collection of essays and lectures, *White Man, Listen!* (1957).

Richard Wright

Wright's last novel published in his lifetime, was *The Long Dream* (1958), the first part of a projected trilogy of works focusing on the story of Tyree Tucker, a corrupt, Southern black undertaker, and his son Fishbelly, who try to escape the brutality of racism. The book was poorly received in the United States, especially among blacks, who accused Wright of being out of touch with the progressive changes taking place there between blacks and whites.

Even in his adopted country of France, Wright was beginning to recognize the painful face of racial inequality, as millions of blacks from French colonies such as Algeria flooded into France to take menial jobs and live in slums. Wright thought he might try living in England but got caught up in that country's immigration laws, which limited the number of people of color allowed in as residents. Ellen, who now had a career as a literary agent, stayed behind with the children and Wright shuttled back and forth across the English Channel to be with his family.

By 1960, Wright found comfort in the composing of Japanese *haiku*, a precise, three-line form of poetry noted for its elegant simplicity. He wrote some 4,000 of the poems and thought of looking for a publisher.* His pursuits were cut short in November by stomach troubles, which laid him up for a week. After a brief recovery, Wright took ill with the flu, digestive problems and dizzy spells. He was hospitalized and put on penicillin, which seemed to clear things up. Thus it was a shock to everyone when, on the night of November 28, Wright suffered a heart attack and died. He was 52 years old.

Richard Wright died on the eve of the most explosive period of the civil rights movement. "[I]t was a movement he had foreseen," wrote biographer Williams. "Indeed, in many ways he helped to spur it."

Other American writers from 1900 to 1950, such as London and Anderson, had dealt with how society was changing; Wright wrote of how society needed change. Fitzgerald and Hemingway had given us the stories of familiar white, Anglo-Saxon, Protestant Americans, both at home and abroad; Wright took us into the heart of the ghetto and showed us the lives of black Americans—something no one had dared do before. In doing so he opened up

---

* Although the book Wright envisioned was never published, some of the poems have since appeared in *Ebony* magazine, in collections of black poetry and in biographies of Wright.

the field for other black writers who followed, such as James Baldwin and Ralph Ellison.

Moreover, as Williams points out, Wright broadened our awareness of people of color from all corners of the globe and "might be considered one of the originators of the concept of the 'Third World.'" Written off and largely forgotten by his generation, Wright is now recognized as one of America's most visionary writers. He believed in the day when people of all races would be treated with respect, if for no other reason than that they demanded it. Wright understood the power and universality of this basic human need.

"I do hope that you continue to dig into the rich materials of Negro life and lift them up for all to see," Wright stated in a letter to poet and friend, Owen Dodson.* "[Y]ou'll be doing more than holding up Negro life for others to see, but you will be holding up human life in all its forms for all to see. The more we dig into Negro life, the more we are digging into human life."

---

* Published in *Richard Wright: Impressions and Perspectives*, edited by David Ray and Robert M. Farnsworth (Ann Arbor: University of Michigan Press, 1973).

Chronology

September 4, 1908	born on a farm near Natchez, Mississippi
1914	father Nathan deserts family in Memphis, Tennessee, forcing them to move in with a variety of relatives
1924–25	"The Voodoo of Hell's Half Acre," his first short story, is published; graduates from Smith-Robinson Public School as class valedictorian
1927	moves to Chicago and begins reading at night in the public library
1932	joins the Communist Party
1938	first novel, *Uncle Tom's Children*, published
1939	Marries Dhima Meadman
1940–41	*Native Son* published; marries Ellen Poplar
1945	his first autobiography, *Black Boy*, published
1947	leaves America and moves to France
1953–55	visits Africa and Asia
November 28, 1960	dies of a heart attack in Paris, France

Further Reading

Wright's Works
Native Son (New York: Perennial Library, 1987). Wright's controversial first novel that shocked the reading public and helped shape modern black literature. This edition includes Wright's revealing essay, "How Bigger Was Born."

Black Boy (New York: Harper & Row, 1945). Wright's account of his early years in the South.

American Hunger (New York: Harper & Row, 1977). Continuation of Wright's autobiography; includes informative afterword by Michel Fabre.

The Richard Wright Reader, edited by Ellen Wright with Michel Fabre (New York: Harper and Row, 1978). Contains letters, poetry and essays as well as excerpts from Wright's novels and longer works.

Books About Wright
Michel Fabre, *The Unfinished Quest of Richard Wright* (New York: Morrow, 1973). The definitive, adult biography.

Joan Uban, *Richard Wright* (New York: Chelsea House, 1989). Good, juvenile biography.

John A. Williams, *The Most Native of Sons* (Garden City, N.Y.: Doubleday, 1970). A good, concise biography that puts Wright's life in the perspective of the times.

Index

Bold numbers indicate main headings; *italic* numbers indicate illustrations and captions; numbers followed by *"t"* indicate chronology.

133

Index

Index

Index

Index

Index